# Winning the War Within!

## HOW TO CHOOSE RIGHT OVER WRONG
## AND EXPERIENCE TRUE SUCCESS

## TRACIE PELOTTE

Italics in scripture quotations reflect the author's added emphasis.

26 25 24 23 22     6 5 4 3 2

ISBN: 13 978-1-937250-87-4

*Winning the War Within!—*
*How to Choose Right Over Wrong and Experience True Success*
Copyright © 2020 by Tracie Pelotte

For additional copies email: winningthewarwithin.bk.pelotte@gmail.com

Published by:    Ken and Tracie Pelotte
                 Tulsa, OK 74145

Cover design by Mandy Pelotte

Printed in the United States of America

# Acknowledgements

The first and most important acknowledgement belongs to my Father God and Lord Jesus Christ! He challenged and enabled me to do things I never thought I could. I am forever grateful to Him for His faithfulness!

To my husband Ken, my greatest encourager on earth, many thanks. I'm so grateful for your support and help with this book and gentle push to keep me going.

To my kids; Clayton, Corina, Jeremy and Jessica, you mean the world to me. Thank you for your big part in helping me, pushing me, and encouraging me in this project. And, to my son-in-law Sam Parker and my daughters-in-law Ashlyn and Mandy, I really appreciate how you jumped on board with your help and support. Mandy, thank you for the incredible job you did on the cover of this book. I'm so very proud and grateful to all of you!

Thank you Mom, Ellyn Aaron, for taking the time to make morning phone appointments with me to help fine-tune the final draft. Your wisdom and intelligence is greatly appreciated. I held tight to the encouraging line you told me from the very beginning. It went something like, "Make sure you don't stop. Stay with it and finish it."

To my friend, Jayne Sleeter, for all your encouragement, help and direction with each step in getting this book published. You were truly a Godsend. And thank you to my friend, Jewell Griffith, for inspiring me and sharing your wisdom and knowledge in writing.

To my dear niece, Angelina Chea, whom I emailed the final manuscript before it was published in hopes it would bless and direct her in her recent call from God into a deeper walk and commitment to Him. I appreciate your positive feedback. It was a great confirmation.

# Contents

# Introduction

In my several years of jail ministry, I have seen the bondage of so many behind bars because of the lack of understanding of their value and who their real enemy is. Yet a lot of people on the "outside," while not physically imprisoned, are in the same kind of emotional and mental prison, with a distorted view of themselves and a sense they cannot measure up. It seems to be a constant battle.

You or someone you know may be dealing with these frustrating feelings. My desire is to bring hope and assurance to you with this book. Basically, I want you to grasp, not just believe, what's been done for you. This is the only way you can enjoy a balanced, godly life and win the war that's been raging within you.

Perhaps you just need to change the order of your thoughts or the way you have been approaching things. Or you may just need to learn your true structure and the relationship between your spirit, your soul, and your body—how the real you (your spirit) relates to God; and how another part of you (your flesh) does not. Once you truly understand how to yield to the part—the real you—that gives you such a beautiful relationship with your Maker through His Son, Jesus Christ, and you refuse to yield to the part (your flesh) that tries to pull you away from Him, and live based on that understanding, you can become much more than you ever thought you could be. And you'll realize that anyone can achieve this.

To be totally free and complete is when you go beyond just gaining hope for yourself, and develop a hope for all humanity.

I am a living testimony of what this truth can do. I grew up with a distorted self-view, despising myself, due to abuse in my childhood that my parents didn't even know about. Actually, no one did. I was too confused, afraid, and embarrassed to tell anyone, until someone finally asked me about it when I was around 13. I just burst into tears, after releasing what was bottled up for years. It was a relief to get it out, but also the problems such abuse created were overwhelming. Even after I completely committed my life to the Lord, I found myself coming up against these issues.

Although I stayed committed to Him and grew in other areas, I just couldn't seem to break free of this chain. Then, unexpectedly, the Lord opened up an opportunity for me to attend a nine-month Bible school course, by someone anonymously paying my way. As I immersed myself in the scriptural teaching and in prayer and worship, my understanding began to open up in this area of distortion in how we view ourselves. The more I saw in the Word of God, the freer I became. I saw truth, and it's truth that makes us free. (John 8:32.) The exciting thing is the more we seek Him, the more truth is revealed.

After graduating from Domata School of Ministry, I began to do studies on what Scriptures say about certain subjects— anger, strife, the tongue, and obedience, among others—which led me to the study of the flesh and the spirit. It dawned on me that it all boils down to this subject.

I cannot fully express just how much this project has helped me in my personal life as I more consistently put these things I believe the Lord showed me into practice. As I got deeper into this study, I felt a strong impression in my heart and through other confirmations that this was to become a book, a tool to help set people free, as it has me.

I purposely started from scratch, giving a run-through of the gospel, not only because it is my hope that you will receive salvation through this message if you never have before, but also because it's important to get the whole picture. Are you already a Christian? Please be patient and know that it's always good to go back to the basics and remember the pure, simple gospel. It's mighty powerful! It is so important to grasp the fundamentals I will lay out in the next few chapters. But just hold on; once we have laid the foundation I will come back to the war between the flesh and the spirit and how to win in the war!

My prayer is that when you finish this book, you won't just put it down and forget about the biblical instruction that has the potential to change your life, but you'll begin practicing what you learned and go deeper into the Word of God and in your relationship with Him.

## Succeed and Progress

I also pray that you will come to know the truth that God is no respecter of persons. (Acts 10:34.) If the formula God has given works for one, it will work for all. The only difference is whether or not we put it into practice. The good news is our will and determination to live a disciplined life can be strengthened, but it takes a quality decision. You must at least be "willing to be willing."

Don't be afraid of the word *discipline*. In all reality, it's simply an action that leads to complete security. The confirmation of this truth came to me when my son was about five years old. We were out in public, probably in a store, and he decided to misbehave, even after warnings. So, I told him that when we got home he was going to get in trouble. Well, after we arrived at our house, I began to do some chores and reprimanding him completely slipped my mind. A short time later he came to me and whispered in my ear, "You forgot to discipline me." I was shocked, but I realized how he needed that security. This happened with him and his younger sibling on several occasions.

Another time when I was young and with my dad, I remember talking disrespectfully to him, then going to my room feeling so upset at myself, and I thought, "Why doesn't he just spank me?" I'm not talking about punishing yourself. I'm talking about setting standards and guidelines, and not letting yourself break them. My kids and I just wanted the reinforcement that it wasn't okay to step over the line of safety.

As parents set boundaries and apply discipline when their children overstep them, we can learn to set boundaries on ourselves and then watch ourselves succeed and progress into all the good things God intended for us.

God is faithful. He does not make things too hard for us. He did the hard part by sending His own Son to take the consequences of our sin on Himself through being crucified so that we could go free. So be at ease and rest in that truth. And remind yourself each day that God is working in you not just to *want* to do the things that please Him, but also to actually *do* the things that please Him. (Philippians 2:13.) God has not left us to do this on our own. He's always there, providing more than we realize, to see us through every situation in life.

# CHAPTER 1

# How and Where It All Started

To understand the real battle going on inside of you between your flesh and spirit, it's important to understand your whole being and how you're made up of three parts. First Thessalonians 5:23 tells us that those three parts are spirit, soul, and body.

> **The very God of peace sanctify you wholly; and I pray God your whole *spirit and soul and body* be preserved blameless unto the coming of our Lord Jesus Christ.** (KJV)

The real you is your spirit. You live in a body that is the house for your spirit. The body also is called your flesh. And you have a soul. Luke 21:19 shows us that your soul is something you possess. Your soul consists of your mind, will, and emotions. It's your individual personality. It can be hard to distinguish the difference between the spirit and soul. Only through the power and life of the Word of God can the difference be revealed. (Hebrews 4:12.)

We are also told in the Word that when Christians are absent from their body they are present with the Lord. (2 Corinthians 5:8.) But when a person dies, obviously their body doesn't go anywhere. Eventually, it just returns to dust from which it was created. (Genesis 3:19.) This is talking about our earthly bodies. Another part of our being does go someplace when our bodies die—our spirit and soul.

Our spirit and soul are like a battery that keeps the body functioning. Take the spirit and soul out and the body quits working (James 2:26), except, unlike a battery, the spirit and soul never die.

This also can be compared to an egg with its three parts. Inside is what really matters. The shell just preserves it until it becomes a chicken or someone's breakfast. Similarly, our bodies preserve us while here on earth.

Of the three, your spirit is the most important. The soul gives life and action to your body, as we see in animals. With your spirit, however, you can soar in life and relate to God. Jesus explained it in John 4:24: "God is a Spirit: and they that worship him must worship him in spirit and in truth" (KJV). Your soul is what you use to decide which you're going to follow, or obey—your spirit or your flesh.

We were created in the image of God (Genesis 1:26), so in the beginning when He created us, everything about us—spirit, soul, and body—was perfect. Even though Adam and Eve are the ones who experienced that perfect state before the fall, they represent and were the start of the human race, of which we're all a part. We are their offspring.

After Adam and Eve were created, God told them that they could eat of any tree in the beautiful, luxurious garden He placed them in except for the tree of the knowledge of good and evil. (Genesis 2:16–17.) This was their chance to show their love for God. Obedience demonstrates our faith in God and our love for Him. Jesus said it in John 14:15, "If you love Me, keep My commandments." This was also their opportunity to choose for themselves who they wanted to serve. Romans 6:16 says, "Know ye not, that to whom ye yield yourselves servants to obey, his servants ye are to whom ye obey; whether of sin unto death or of obedience [to God] unto righteousness?" (KJV).

God gave Adam and Eve far above what they could ever require or want. Everything was perfect. They had no need for the tree they were told to stay away from. For them, it was all about a challenge. God told them they would die if they ate of that tree. When the enemy (the devil, also called Satan) through the serpent, came to tempt Eve to go ahead and eat of it, he told her that she wouldn't die but that her eyes would be opened and she "would be like God, knowing good and evil" (Genesis 3:5). Just like you and me, Eve had to decide whom she was going to believe.

God and the serpent were saying two different things. Eve's big mistake was that she stayed there and listened and studied the tree, which only caused her desire for it to grow. What if she had, instead, kept her focus on all the great things God had created and given to them? What if she had held tightly to God's words? The more she focused on the wrong thing, the more the temptation drew her in.

Can you relate to this? I know I can. There was a time when the Lord impressed me not to get involved with a certain guy. I continued to hang around him, thinking that I had full control. It wasn't long at all before I was in a relationship with him that became a bondage that was very difficult to get out of. Big lesson learned.

Since we can say that we all have fallen into temptation, we really can't be bitter against Eve; but it's good to note the example and learn from it.

*It is so important to always consider the source of what is being said; does it line up with the truth of God's Word? If not, refuse to give it any attention.*

As the Bible tells us, Eve heeded the snake and ate the fruit that God told her not to eat. Then she gave it to Adam and he also ate it. Suddenly their eyes were opened and they knew they were naked. (Genesis 3:7.) The first thing they noticed was their flesh. The flesh was immediately contaminated, never again to be the same while in this earthly body. The flesh was now corrupted by the evil and filth that comes from the devil. He was given that right when Adam and Eve chose to believe and obey him rather than God. They handed over to Satan the dominion that God had given them, which made him (Satan) the god of this world—and the war started between our flesh and our spirit. (Romans 7.)

## Work the Ground

Genesis 3 goes on to tell us that because Adam chose to listen to Eve and disobey God, the ground is cursed and "in sorrow . . . you shall eat . . . of it all the days of your life" (v. 17 AMP). From that point on it has taken a lot of work and sweat to keep up the ground. Thorns and thistles continue to come out of it. Yet it's where our food comes from, so it has to be taken care of in order for us to survive physically. It will be this way until our bodies return to the ground. (vv. 18–19.) Remember, only our spirit (the real us) will live on.

Can you see how the cursing of the ground relates to our flesh? Our flesh has been affected by Adam and Eve's choice as well. It makes sense because our bodies (our flesh) were made from the ground.

**Genesis 2:7**

7 The Lᴏʀᴅ God formed man of the dust of the ground, and breathed into his nostrils the breath of life; and man became a living being.

We've got to have our bodies to live here, and we've got to cultivate them (spiritually speaking) just like Adam was told to work the ground for the sake of having food. Carnal thorns and thistles often spring up in different forms in our flesh.

**Galatians 5:19–21**

19 Now the works of the flesh are evident, which are: adultery, fornication, uncleanness, lewdness,

20 idolatry, sorcery, hatred, contentions, jealousies, outbursts of wrath, selfish ambitions, dissensions, heresies,

21 envy, murders, drunkenness, revelries, and the like.

Just as with weeds, these fleshly works cannot be tolerated. So, when any of them arise in our thoughts (that's where it all starts), immediately we should say to ourselves, "It's time to till the ground." Uproot the weeds. Get ahold of them before they grow into action and cause damage. Immediately reject what's not right and forget about it by going on to something else, something that *is* right. If Eve had done that, what a different world this would be!

Another tree that Adam and Eve had the liberty to eat from was the tree of life. If they had eaten of that tree *before* they fell, it would have been Heaven on earth from that day on into eternity. It would have been quite the opposite if they would have eaten from that tree *after* their fall—they would have lived forever in their now devastated, darkened, and corrupted state. So God in His love and mercy sent them out of the garden and stationed Angels and a flaming sword at the east of the garden to guard it so Adam and Eve could not go back in and eat of it. (Genesis 3:24.) God had a plan to fix the mess they were in, which caused this to be only a temporary state and after that, to live forever with everything perfect as God intended.

So, from the very onset, we see that God is good! He gives the best, He protects and cares for us, and He fixes the messes we make.

## Law and Grace

Adam and Eve began to have children and as the human race grew, sin grew as well. People became so evil and corrupt. Even though they had a conscience and were aware their behavior was not right, they were unaware that it was actually disobedience and sin. Here's an example that you may relate to.

When we see our toddlers starting to become more aware of what they're doing, we know it's time to start training them about right and wrong; but until we start teaching them, laying down some rules, we can't give consequences, and we can't really judge them as disobedient (or in sin). It was the same before God gave the law to Moses. (Exodus 31:18; Deuteronomy 9:10.) The people knew something wasn't right about their behavior, but it wasn't sin to them until they were told not to behave that way.

**Romans 5:13** NLT

13 **Yes, people sinned even before the law was given. But it was not counted as sin because there was not yet any law to break.**

**Romans 7:7** NLT

7 **Am I suggesting that the law of God is sinful? Of course not! In fact, it was the law that showed me my sin. I would never have known that coveting is wrong if the law had not said, "You must not covet."**

So coveting (or lust) was already happening on earth, but it wasn't revealed or understood to be sin until they were told not to covet (or lust). Even Jesus said when He was here on earth, "If I had not come and spoken to them, they would have no sin, but now they have no excuse for their sin." (John 15:22). He was talking about people in the world who rejected Him.

Now, although the law didn't come until after the flood that God brought on the earth because of humanity's great wickedness (Genesis 6:5–6,17), the people were warned ahead of time by Noah, "a preacher of righteousness" (2 Peter 2:5). Also Noah's lifestyle, according to Genesis 6:9, and his display of faith and trust in God in building the ark before seeing the rain or clouds, said much to the people around him. That alone exposed their error. (Hebrews 11:7.) But they obviously didn't heed him, because only Noah and his family were saved from the devastation. Evidently they, too, were without excuse.

The apostle Paul tells us in Galatians 3:19 that the law was added because of transgressions (sins) until Jesus came. Verses 24 and 25 explain, "The law was our schoolmaster to bring us unto Christ, that we might be justified by faith. But after that faith is come, we are no longer under a schoolmaster" (KJV). Because of the flesh, there was no one who was able to fully keep the law. So, the law was preparation for us to be ready to receive Christ. Paul also describes this in the book of Romans.

Romans 3:19–24

19 Now we know that whatever the law says, it says to those who are under the law, that every mouth may be stopped, and all the world may become guilty before God.

20 Therefore by the deeds of the law no flesh will be justified in His sight, for by the law is the knowledge of sin.

21 But now the righteousness of God apart from the law is revealed, being witnessed by the Law and the Prophets,

22 even the righteousness of God, through faith in Jesus Christ, to all and on all who believe. For there is no difference;

23 for all have sinned and fall short of the glory of God,

24 being justified freely by His grace through the redemption that is in Christ Jesus.

Look also at Galatians 3:11: "But that no man is justified by the law in the sight of God, it is evident: for, The just shall live by faith" (KJV).

The law helped us to see just how desperately we needed a Savior. Even from "before the foundation of the world," sending us a Savior was always God's plan. (1 Peter 1:20 KJV.)

# Jump In on the Winning Side

We (the human race) were in a mess. Yet even in the midst of that mess, God's love for us was so great that He sent His own Son, Jesus, to set us free from the bondage of sin and darkness. God sent Him to take the punishment that we deserved; to win back the authority for us that we lost through the fall in the garden. (Genesis 3.)

Jesus came down and became flesh to set an example and relate to all we face in the flesh. In order for Him to pay the penalty for our sins, however, He had to live a sinless, perfect life—in the flesh—and that He did. Then He had to offer His perfect life on the cross, as He took on Himself our sins and imperfections. He suffered like none other. He was beaten so badly, He was beyond recognition.

**Isaiah 53:4,5**

4  Surely He has borne our griefs and carried our sorrows; yet we esteemed Him stricken, smitten by God, and afflicted.

5  But He was wounded for our transgressions, He was bruised for our iniquities; the chastisement for our peace was upon Him, and by His stripes we are healed.

Another Bible translation for this scripture says:

The fact is, it was our suffering He took on Himself; He bore our pain. But we thought that God was punishing Him, that God was beating Him for something He did. But He was being punished for what we did. He was crushed because of our guilt. He took the punishment we deserved, and this brought us peace. We were healed because of His pain. (ERV)

Jesus went through what He did to completely free us, not just from sins but from anything that would oppress us, such as sickness, discouragement, distress, fear, poverty, and the pressure of upholding the law. They hung Jesus up on a cross by nailing His hands and feet to it. At any moment He could have avoided it all by calling down a regiment of angels from Heaven. (Matthew 26:53.) Yet He allowed the Romans and Jews to do it to set us free from the curse.

**Galatians 3:13,14**

13 Christ has redeemed us from the curse of the law, having become a curse for us (for it is written, "Cursed is everyone who hangs on a tree"),

14 that the blessing of Abraham might come upon the Gentiles in Christ Jesus, that we might receive the promise of the Spirit through faith.

Deuteronomy 28 shows us the blessings for keeping the law and the curses (consequences) for not keeping the law. Once you invite Jesus into your heart and receive Him as your Lord and Savior, you are free from the curses, and the blessings automatically belong to you. The enemy (Satan) will try to make you think otherwise, but you've got to stand firm on the truth that you know.

One truth is that three days after Jesus died, God raised Him from the dead, to complete the work. Romans 4:25 tells us that He was delivered for our offenses and was raised again for our justification "so that we would be made acceptable to God" (CEV). Jesus was put to death for our sins, but God raising Him up from the dead is what justified us, proclaimed us as innocent, "not guilty" before God.

Before Jesus shed His blood on the cross, only the high priest, after a thorough cleansing process, could enter into the Holy of Holies in the temple. Now we have free access into God's presence because of what Jesus did for us.

The thought of blood might seem gory to some, but it's meant to be looked at as our natural supply of life for our flesh. Since sin entered the world, our human nature became dirty and impure. That was the reason for sacrifices—so that the blood of a clean animal could temporarily cover the sin, to keep people alive, by making a way for the high priest to approach God once a year on behalf of the sins of all the people.

Leviticus 17:11 says, "For the life of the flesh is in the blood, and I have given it to you upon the altar to make atonement for your souls; it is the blood that makes atonement for the soul." The way everything was set up back before Jesus came was meant to be in a pattern of what was to come. So, although this verse is talking about the earthly tabernacle that was set up and the blood of particular animals, it was an example of Jesus becoming the spotless Lamb that was to be sacrificed.

**Hebrews 9:13,14 KJV**

**13 For if the blood of bulls and of goats, and the ashes of an heifer sprinkling the unclean, sanctifieth to the purifying of the flesh:**

**14** how much more shall the blood of Christ, who through the eternal Spirit offered himself without spot to God, purge your conscience from dead works to serve the living God?

Jesus was the final and perfect sacrifice that took away the sins of the people, not just cover them for a short time as the blood of animals had done. Now His purifying blood is available not only for initial salvation, but also for times of slipping up along the way. First John 1:9 says, "If we confess our sins, He is faithful and just to forgive us our sins and to cleanse us from all unrighteousness."

## The Gift of God

Not only does the blood of Jesus wash away our sins and enable us to approach God 24/7, but it also gives us a clear, guiltless conscience, as we just saw in Hebrews 9, at the end of verse 14. The writer of Hebrews continues:

**Hebrews 9:22–24** KJV

**22** Almost all things are by the law purged with blood; and without shedding of blood is no remission.

**23** It was therefore necessary that the patterns of things in the heavens should be purified with these; but the heavenly things themselves with better sacrifices than these.

**24** For Christ is not entered into the holy places made with hands, which are the figures of the true; but into heaven itself, now to appear in the presence of God for us.

I like the way Paul summed it up in the book of Romans:

**Romans 5:11,12,18–21** KJV

11 And not only so, but we also joy in God through our Lord Jesus Christ, by whom we have now received the atonement.

12 Wherefore, as by one man sin entered into the world, and death by sin; and so death passed upon all men, for that all have sinned . . .

18 Therefore as by the offense of one judgment came upon all men to condemnation; even so by the righteousness of one the free gift came upon all men unto justification of life.

19 For as by one man's disobedience many were made sinners, so by the obedience of one shall many be made righteous.

20 Moreover the law entered, that the offense might abound. But where sin abounded, grace did much more abound:

21 That as sin hath reigned unto death, even so might grace reign through righteousness unto eternal life by Jesus Christ our Lord.

Paul goes on to say, "For the wages of sin is death; but the gift of God is eternal life through Jesus Christ our Lord" (Romans 6:23 KJV).

The only part that we have to play to make this whole plan work for us is to simply believe and confess that this gospel is true, and that Jesus is Lord. And choose to let Him be the Lord over our lives.

**Romans 10:9,10**

9 If you confess with your mouth the Lord Jesus and believe in your heart that God has raised Him from the dead, you will be saved.

10 For with the heart one believes unto righteousness, and with the mouth confession is made unto salvation.

When you call "on the name of the Lord," you'll be saved. (v. 13.) And you'll be instantly switched to the winning side, with the promise of spending eternity in Heaven as your reward that you didn't even have to earn.

**Ephesians 2:8**

8  **By grace you have been saved through faith, and that not of yourselves; it is the gift of God.**

It's really that simple. In this world nothing is free, but remember that this gift did not come from the world; and it is free. It came from the Giver of life Himself.

# CHAPTER 3

# Countless Benefits

Going to Bible school was an awesome privilege and experience that changed my life in so many ways. The main reason my life changed was I began to realize more about what I have and who I am in Christ as a born-again believer. It totally built up my level of confidence. For instance, symptoms of sickness hit my body about five different times during that year. In the past, I would have responded by accepting them and going with the way I felt. However, armed with my newfound understanding of the authority we have been given in Christ, I boldly rejected them and saw them leave. I was like one of those bug lights that zaps the bugs when they land on it. I felt so illuminated inside; I knew that sickness just couldn't remain on my body if I would act on the truth I had learned.

Although we are immediately equipped with power and authority when we accept Christ (Luke 10:19), it takes seeking Him and growing in Him to understand and walk in that reality. I had already been a Christian for several years, but I didn't know how to operate in that freedom and authority that Christ gave me. Spending all that time at Bible school sitting under the teaching of the Word and worshiping God made a huge difference. Hearing God's Word builds our faith, and faith is how we receive from God. Faith is expecting, being totally convinced, regardless of thoughts, feelings, and circumstances. And faith must remain until the manifestation shows up.

My oldest daughter and son-in-law had their car stolen out of their driveway one night. It wasn't until three months later that they received a call from a police officer, who told them that the police had found their car. They also had $2,000 worth of weightlifting equipment that was still in the car and unharmed. After that long you'd think it was hopeless. But I imagine, in this circumstance, if it was found within days, the credit could have been given to the police. But three months later? You know it was God!

Another cool thing about this is God took care of them in the waiting. Someone had lent them a much nicer car to drive; plus, the gym they work out at had replaced most of the equipment. They donated that equipment after they received their own back. Bottom line—it's not over till it's over. Keep trusting; keep believing.

Becoming born again (receiving Jesus in your life) is amazing and indescribable. Second Corinthians 5:17 talks about it like this: "If any man [or woman] be *in Christ*, he is a new creature: old things are passed away; behold, all things become new" (KJV). You become brand-new on the inside. You begin to see things in a different light. Somehow, even creation and the natural scenery become more beautiful.

If being *in Christ* seems mysterious to you, Colossians 1:27 makes it clear: "The mystery in a nutshell is just this: Christ is in you, so therefore you can look forward to sharing in God's glory. It's that simple" (MSG).

We have so many benefits as believers who are in Christ. Here are a few more:

This is the covenant that I will make with them after those days, saith the Lord, I will put my laws into their hearts, and in their minds will I write them; and their sins and iniquities will I remember no more. Now where remission of these is, there is no more offering for sin.

Hebrews 10:19–22 KJV

19 Having therefore, brethren, boldness to enter into the holiest by the blood of Jesus,

20 by a new and living way, which he hath consecrated for us, through the veil, that is to say, his flesh;

21 and having a high priest over the house of God;

22 let us draw near with a true heart in full assurance of faith, having our hearts sprinkled from an evil conscience, and our bodies washed with pure water.

This scripture passage shows us that after we receive Jesus, not only do we have access into the throne room of God, but also something takes place on the inside of us. We have a new "resident" within, and through Him our spirit has become connected with God, like a father and son or daughter, because that's what we really are now—we've been adopted into God's family. Only, this adoption is not quite like any typical adoption here on earth. This one is supernatural. We become full blood family relatives, by the blood of Jesus.

We (on the inside) become like our Father God. That's why we can never truly enjoy sin again after we've been born again. Our flesh will try to rise up and crave sin at times because that part of us has not been renewed, but our spirit (the real us) grieves over sin. Just like kids can't help but imitate their parents and grow up thinking like them, that's how we are with God, on the inside.

**Romans 8:14–17**

14 For as many as are led by the Spirit of God, these are sons of God.

15 For you did not receive the spirit of bondage again to fear, but you received the Spirit of adoption by whom we cry out, "Abba, Father."

16 The Spirit Himself bears witness with our spirit that we are the children of God,

17 and if children, then heirs—heirs of God and joint heirs with Christ, if indeed we suffer with Him, that we may also be glorified together.

Once we receive the knowledge of the truth and accept Jesus as our Lord and Savior, we become enlightened. No longer are we in the dark. Adam and Eve were told by God that if they ate of the tree of the knowledge of good and evil that they would die. That death was a spiritual death, which put them in darkness once they ate of that tree (eventually they did die physically too because of that). But now we've been made spiritually alive, no longer bound by the chains that held us or by the lifestyle that imprisoned us. Our eyes have become opened to reality.

Isaiah 42:6–7 tells us,

6 I, the LORD, have called You in righteousness, and will hold Your hand; I will keep You and give You as a covenant to the people, as a light to the Gentiles,

7 to open blind eyes, to bring out prisoners from the prison, those who sit in darkness from the prison house.

This scripture passage is talking about God sending Jesus to deliver us out of bondage and darkness, to open our eyes to the truth. Some other verses concerning us say:

1 Peter 2:9 KJV

9 Ye are a chosen generation, a royal priesthood, a holy nation, a peculiar people; that ye should show forth the praises of him who hath called you out of darkness into his marvelous light.

2 Corinthians 4:6,7 KJV

6 God, who commanded the light to shine out of darkness, hath shined in our hearts, to give the light of the knowledge of the glory of God in the face of Jesus Christ.

7 But we have this treasure in earthen vessels, that the excellency of the power may be of God, and not of us.

It's obvious because of the frailty of our flesh, which is our earthen vessel, that it's all God's doing. All credit and glory go to Him.

## The Evidence of Faith

As you can see, the benefits of being in Christ are so wonderful and numerous. The following passage reveals their importance, as it tells us to not forget them.

Psalm 103:2–5

2 Bless the LORD, O my soul,
   And forget not all His benefits:

3 Who forgives all your iniquities,
   Who heals all your diseases,

4 Who redeems your life from destruction,
   Who crowns you with lovingkindness and tender mercies,

5 Who satisfies your mouth with good things,
   So that your youth is renewed like the eagle's.

We should always remind ourselves that these things belong to us because we are in Christ. This is like our written contract; written in blood (literally).

Notice that the devil offers the complete opposite. He steals, kills, and destroys. (John 10:10.) When he tries to steal these facts from you or if he tries to convince you that you don't have a right to these benefits, you have this concrete evidence to stand on—your faith in this scripture. (Hebrews 11:1.) But you have to know your benefits, and you need to verbally tell him what they are. He can't take advantage of you if he knows you're on to him, because you know the truth and believe it.

The more you seek the Lord wholeheartedly, the more you learn about your benefits and what and who you now have on the inside of you. And the more you realize that, the more confident you become. There's so much more than we can comprehend.

Romans 8:18 says, "For I consider that the sufferings of this present time are not worthy to be compared with the glory which shall be revealed *in* us." We'll see it all when Jesus comes again (1 Thessalonians 4:16–17), and no doubt we'll be beyond amazed. I already feel that way each time I discover more.

My daughter first discovered the believer's authority in Christ during the year I attended Domata. She was 5 years old at the time and she got so sick one day that she hardly ate. When I tucked her in bed that night, I told her she would wake up hungry. I wasn't just hoping; I understood that I had that authority as a child of God. The next morning, the first thing she said was, "My tummy hurts, but this time because it's hungry." She didn't get hit with the flu again until she was ten years old. She spiked a fever one evening, but with boldness she took authority herself and said, "Tomorrow I will not have this fever!" She slept well and woke up fever free!

I wish I could tell you that it happens that way every time we're attacked in our bodies. Some things take a longer process to develop the faith we need to receive. Sometimes we're just not quite there. But we must hold on to God's Word as the ultimate truth no matter how we feel, and not give up. We must remain in expectation. (There is more on this topic in chapter 15.)

As you continue to see or acknowledge "every good thing which is in you in Christ Jesus," your faith will become more effective. (Philemon 1:6.) Your faith is the victory (1 John 5:4), and it's what you need to get anything accomplished in and for the kingdom of God. No wonder the enemy tries his best to keep us from seeing all that we are equipped with in Christ!

# CHAPTER 4

# The Problem Causers

Once you've been made new on the inside (became born again), everything is different and seems perfect. You've never been so happy. You're overwhelmed with the peace and joy of the Lord. As time goes by, however, you'll find that you'll come up against opposition, and wonder what happened. The explanation is in the Word of God, where we can find all of our answers.

Our opposition is from the devil, and the flesh. The devil, whose name originally was Lucifer, was a beautiful angel created by God. But his beauty went to his head (Ezekiel 28:17), as he thought he should be in a place above God. Therefore, he was kicked out of Heaven and became the enemy, Satan—the ruler of darkness.

**Isaiah 14:12–15 KJV**

12 How art thou fallen from heaven, O Lucifer, son of the morning! how art thou cut down to the ground, which didst weaken the nations!

13 For thou hast said in thine heart, I will ascend into heaven, I will exalt my throne above the stars of God: I will sit also upon the mount of the congregation, in the sides of the north:

14 I will ascend above the heights of the clouds; I will be like the most High.

15 Yet thou shalt be brought down to hell, to the sides of the pit.

Look at the illustration Jesus gives us in Mark 4 about the oppositions we come up against. First, Jesus tells it in a parable to the whole crowd gathered on the beach to listen to Him teach as He sat in a fishing boat a little ways from shore.

Mark 4:3–9

3 "Listen! Behold, a sower went out to sow.

4 And it happened, as he sowed, that some seed fell by the way side; and the birds of the air came and devoured it.

5 Some fell on stony ground, where it did not have much earth; and immediately it sprang up because it had no depth of earth.

6 But when the sun was up it was scorched, and because it had no root it withered away.

7 And some seed fell among thorns; and the thorns grew up and choked it, and it yielded no crop.

8 But other seed fell on good ground and yielded a crop that sprang up, increased and produced: some thirtyfold, some sixty, and some a hundred."

9 And He said to them, 'He who has ears to hear, let him hear!'"

Then Jesus later explains the meaning to His disciples because they asked Him about it.

Mark 4:14–20

14 "The sower sows the word.

15 And these are the ones by the wayside where the word is sown. When they hear, Satan comes immediately and takes away the word that was sown in their hearts.

16 These likewise are the ones sown on stony ground who, when they hear the word, immediately receive it with gladness;

17 and they have no root in themselves, and so endure only for a time. Afterward, when tribulation or persecution arises for the word's sake, immediately they stumble.

18 "Now these are the ones sown among thorns; they are the ones who hear the word,

19 and the cares of this world, the deceitfulness of riches, and the desires for other things entering in choke the word, and it becomes unfruitful.

20 But these are the ones sown on good ground, those who hear the word, accept it, and bear fruit: some thirtyfold, some sixty, and some a hundred."

Notice in verse 17 that the affliction or persecution comes because the enemy is after the Word that's in your heart. The Bible tells us to keep or guard our hearts with all diligence. (Proverbs 4:23.) So, you need not get offended and take it personally when others treat you wrong, or you come up against various struggles, such as physical or financial. It's not about you; it's about a real spiritual warfare going on between Light and darkness.

Each person on this earth is on one of those two sides. There is no in-between or sidelines to just sit and watch. But if you have chosen to follow Christ, as long as you hang on to your faith in the Word (Bible) that God's given to you, you can rest assured that you will remain on the winning side. (Romans 12:3.)

We already know the end results. Many scriptures in the Word tell us and reveal which side wins. One is Revelation 12:10–11.

10 Then I heard a loud voice saying in heaven, "Now salvation, and strength, and the kingdom of our God, and the power of his Christ have come, for the accuser of our brethren, who accused them before our God day and night, has been cast down.

**11** And they overcame him by the blood of the Lamb and by the word of their testimony, and they did not love their lives to the death."

Let the Word of God and all that He's done for you be your testimony.

## Dressed to Win

You'll notice that often after enjoying the wonderful feeling of spending time in the presence of God, the enemy, Satan, will present subtle attacks to you, such as temptations, doubts, and discouragement, because he wants to steal what you just received from the Lord. We always receive something when we spend time with God and in His Word—strength, growth, revelation, and more to give out to others, as well as peace, joy, and further understanding of God's love for us. It's so important to realize that in the middle of the emotion, although it feels great at the time, we need to prepare to hold tightly to our commitment when the feelings let up. We can't live according to how we feel.

God has not left us defenseless. He has given us a perfect spiritual armor to wear that nothing can penetrate and that cannot fail, when worn correctly. Ephesians 6:10 tells us to "be strong in the Lord and in the power of His might." The instructions for being strong in the Lord are well laid out in the following description on how to put on His armor.

Ephesians 6:11, 14–17 KJV

**11** Put on the whole armour of God, that ye may be able to stand against the wiles of the devil. . . .

14 Stand therefore, having your loins girt about with truth, and having on the breastplate of righteousness;

15 And your feet shod with the preparation of the gospel of peace;

16 Above all, taking the shield of faith, wherewith ye shall be able to quench all the fiery darts of the wicked.

17 And take the helmet of salvation, and the sword of the Spirit, which is the Word of God.

According to this passage, when opposition comes, here's what you do. Recognize what it's really about; guard against it and resist it immediately with your faith as your shield; know the truth and hold on to it ever so tightly, knowing it's what holds everything else together; and keep your heart guarded with the knowledge that you're in right standing with God because of Jesus (which will help you to live righteously). And have your feet ready to go forward for the sake (or defense) of the gospel of peace, always remembering that you have salvation no matter how you feel or what thoughts try to bombard your mind, with the Word of God continuously coming out your mouth, which will destroy the enemy's plan of attack!

This spiritual armor needs to be on us from the moment we wake up, throughout each day, way before the battle hits. We put it on by praying and by digging into and getting more and more familiar with the Word, getting settled on what exactly you choose to believe, and creating a daily habit of speaking out (meditating on) scriptures, such as:

- The Lord will perfect that which concerns me (Psalm 138:8),

- I shall not die, but live, and declare the works of the Lord (Psalm 118:17),

- The Lord is on my side; I will not fear (Psalm 118:6),

- I have the mind of Christ (1 Corinthians 2:16),

- I am the righteousness of God in Christ
  (2 Corinthians 5:21),

- I am not ashamed of the gospel of Christ
  (Romans 1:16).

It's quite difficult to put on armor in the middle of an attack. You're sure to get hurt. The enemy will certainly take advantage of that. He also will look for any openings to drive his fiery darts into. That's why we are told to put on the *whole* armor of God.

The writer of Hebrews tells us to "hold fast the profession of our faith without wavering," for God is faithful who promised. (Hebrews 10:23.) Above all else, it's our faith that helps us to stand against everything the devil throws at us. (Ephesians 6:16.) So by faith stand firm on the Word you received and the commitment you made, regardless of the circumstances and the emotions you might be experiencing.

One Bible translation calls the Word an "indispensable weapon" (v. 17 MSG). Know that whatever you are going through will pass, but the Word of God stands forever. (Isaiah 40:8.) You can be confident of that with the same confidence that you first received after you were born again.

The Greek word for *confidence* can be translated as "cheerful courage, boldness, assurance."[1] The Bible has much to say about being confident. For instance, Hebrews 10:35 says, "Cast not away therefore your confidence, which hath great recompense of reward" (KJV). Isaiah 30:15 tells us, "In quietness and in confidence shall be your strength" (KJV). And Solomon, the writer of Proverbs, said, "For the LORD will be your confidence, and will keep your foot from being caught" (Proverbs 3:26).

One way to confidently hang on to the Word you've been taught is to practice doing what it says.

James 1:22–25

22 Be doers of the word, and not hearers only, deceiving yourselves.

23 For if any one is a hearer of the word and not a doer, he is like a man observing his natural face in a mirror;

24 for he observes himself, goes away, and immediately forgets what kind of man he was.

25 But he who looks into the perfect law of liberty and continues in it, and is not a forgetful hearer but a doer of the work, this one will be blessed in what he does.

Getting directions to a certain place or even being a passenger doesn't help me to know confidently how to get there. But the more I drive there myself, the more it becomes imbedded in my memory. That's how it works with the Word. The more you obey it, the more it becomes imbedded in you. You're no longer just hearing the directions. Now you know them by heart, and it becomes a natural response for you to do what the Word says.

## Walk This Way

So often we hear people, including some Christians, talk about how God allows or causes bad things to happen to teach or to test people. Nothing could be further from the truth. James 1:13 says, "Let no one say when he is tempted, 'I am tempted by God'; for God cannot be tempted by evil, *nor does*

*He Himself tempt anyone.*" And verse 17 says, "Every good gift and every perfect gift is from above, and comes down from the Father of lights, *with whom there is no variation or shadow of turning.*" God doesn't change. This is the way He is, and always will be.

We also hear some individuals question, "If God loves us so much, why does He allow all these evil things to happen?" Remember that before the fall everything on earth was just the way God had intended for it to be. But God wanted man to choose for himself whether he wanted God to rule on the earth that He gave him. (Psalm 115:16.) And when Adam and Eve chose to obey Satan, they chose to make him rule on this earth. Therefore, Satan's condemnation became our condemnation.

It's not about God saying, "Serve Me or you will go to hell"; it's more like, "Serve Me so you can escape hell." We were all already under condemnation and on our way there. John 3:18 says, "He who believes in [Jesus] is not condemned; but he who does not believe is condemned already." God made an escape route through the sacrifice and resurrection of His Son, Jesus, for all who would believe and accept Him, which completely frees us from condemnation and from Satan's authority over us personally. (John 14:6; Romans 10:13.)

So, instead of looking at it as *all that God is allowing*, look at it as *all that Satan is doing*. God made a way out of Satan's doings for those who will take it—and you only can take it by faith. You still will be attacked as long as you're here on the earth, but just keep in mind Psalm 34:19 that says, "Many are the afflictions of the righteous, *but the LORD delivers him out of them all.*" Not only that, but all those who are in Christ can have peace in the middle of any circumstance. (John 16:33.) That's good news!

It's important to understand that we're not actually fighting against our flesh or anyone else's. Ephesians 6:12 tells us, "For we wrestle not against flesh and blood, but against principalities, against powers, against the rulers of the darkness of this world, against spiritual wickedness in high places" (KJV). Every one of us has flesh, which is like a "bad side" so to speak—but it's not a part of our new nature that we now have because of Christ. (2 Corinthians 5:17.) We have the ability to not allow that side to dominate or have its way.

If you work close to or are friends with people in ministry, and you see them giving in to a fleshly attitude, if you're not careful, you can have trouble receiving from the spiritual gifts in them. You have to learn to distinguish between the flesh and the Spirit. You cannot shut a person down just because you've seen them acting in the flesh. Every one of us has given in to the flesh a time or two, or more like a million times plus, depending on our age. (Romans 7:14–20.)

So, don't beat yourself up or criticize others. Be patient and merciful, just as God is toward you. Thank God for not shutting us down when we've messed up.

Our enemy, then, is the devil, the one who caused the problems we have with our flesh. Our job is to keep the flesh from ruling in our lives and know that the enemy is defeated. He has no power over us. Jesus has given us authority and power over him.

**Luke 10:19** KJV

19 Behold, I give unto you power to tread on serpents and scorpions, and over all the power of the enemy: and nothing shall by any means hurt you.

This scripture was quoted to my dad years ago by the late Reverend Dick Mills, a well-known Bible teacher and preacher. On several occasions after that, my dad found himself within inches of a rattlesnake. One time he was standing on a rock that a snake was under. Another time he was working on some bushes that a snake was in and he ended up face-to-face with it. He also talked of an occasion of tripping over or stepping on one. Yet, he was never harmed by any of them.

Now, my dad did not go looking for these snakes to prove this verse, and neither should we. That would not be wise. Yet, if by accident one appears in our pathway, the power of God can protect us, just as it protected the apostle Paul, who, although he was actually bit by a poisonous snake, wasn't harmed by it. (Acts 28:3–5.) The point is that when we have God's power in our lives, we can destroy Satan's schemes against us—we can come "face-to-face" with him and have the victory.

God's promises are for real. If we'll take them to heart and believe them, they may not always come to pass in the way we might think, but they will come to pass.

Take your stand in the authority you've been given and don't allow the enemy to push you around with discouragement, oppression, fear, or anything else that's not of God. We need to refuse to be intimidated and to choose to be bold as a lion. Every believer has it in them to walk this way.

# CHAPTER 5

# The Right Perspective

Understanding the gospel and grasping what's been done freely for you makes all the difference. You've been put in right standing with God without having done anything, except receive it as a free gift. Second Corinthians 5:21 says, "[God] made [Jesus] who knew no sin to be sin for us, that we might become the righteousness of God in Him." It was free. You would not and could not have been able to do anything to put yourself there.

The more you see and understand that, the easier it is to walk right and do right. It builds a confidence and a peace that can't come from your own works. The most important thing is to have the right perspective on what this is all about. When you realize what you *already* have (as a born-again believer), then it's much easier to do right, rather than trying really hard to do right so that you can have (salvation or approval of God). The pressure has been taken off.

This is a major truth that I grasped while attending Domata. One line quoted in class that really stood out to me was, "Right standing produces right actions." Romans 2:4 says, "Do you despise the riches of his goodness, forbearance, and longsuffering, not knowing that the goodness of God leads you to repentance?" Repentance is simply to have a change of heart, a change in "the way you think and act" (GW), "a radical life-change" (MSG). To *repent* is about turning around and going in a different direction. As you can see in Romans 2:4, it's not condemnation from God that leads us to repent and do what's right, it's His goodness.

A great example of this is in the calling of Simon Peter. Luke 4:38–39 tells how Jesus went into Simon's house and instantly healed his mother-in-law of a high fever. Then in Luke 5:4–10 Jesus performed the miracle of the big catch for Simon, after Simon and his men had fished all night and caught nothing. That's when Simon fell on his knees and said, "Depart from me, for I am a sinful man, O Lord!" (v. 8). It wasn't because of the miracle itself, or else Simon would have done that when his mother-in-law was healed. It was because of the great act of kindness done for him personally.

The overwhelming part for Simon was that he knew he didn't deserve it. Yet Jesus accepted him anyway, telling him not to be afraid because from now on he would catch people. (v. 10.) So Simon repented, left everything, and went right into ministry, following Jesus. (v. 11.)

It seems as though we start off our new life in Christ with that right perspective, because, like Simon, we're so overwhelmed with how God reached out to us while we were in darkness, not even trying to live for Him. It was quite obvious that it had nothing to do with our works. Romans 5:8–10 reveals this:

8 **God commendeth his love toward us, in that, while we were yet sinners, Christ died for us.**

9 **Much more then, being now justified by his blood, we shall be saved from wrath through him.**

10 For if, when we were enemies, we were reconciled to God by the death of his Son, much more, being reconciled, we shall be saved by his life. (KJV)

Yet after a while, a lot of Christians get it twisted and soon start depending on their works to be in right standing with God (which is the natural, fleshly way). That leads to nothing but frustration and discouragement.

We should not be stressing about living right. If we put too much thought into it, it can be overwhelming and even paralyzing. Remember, it's in Spirit and truth that we worship God, and worshiping Him is our lifestyle. (John 4:23–24.) So, all we do should be done in Spirit and in truth. We are called to enjoy our relationship with God and to rest in His promises, through faith. Hebrews 4:3 says, "We which have believed do enter into rest" (KJV). It's so important to cast off all anxiety and to rejoice in how great our God is and how blessed we are to know that He is right there with us—and always will be. His strength is made perfect in our weakness. (2 Corinthians 12:9.)

Galatians 5:1, 4–8 NLT

1 So Christ has truly set us free. Now make sure that you stay free, and don't get tied up again in slavery to the law.

4 For if you are trying to make yourselves right with God by keeping the law, you have been cut off from Christ! You have fallen away from God's grace.

5 But we who live by the Spirit eagerly wait to receive by faith the righteousness God has promised to us.

6 For when we place our faith in Christ Jesus, there is no benefit in being circumcised or being uncircumcised. What is important is faith expressing itself in love.

7 **You were running the race so well. Who has held you back from following the truth?**

8 **It certainly isn't God, for he is the one who called you to freedom.**

I have been tempted now and then to revert to the way that I have thought for years—the thoughts of depending too much on myself instead of depending fully on God and His ability in me, and remembering my position in Christ in which I have been placed. I realize that if I'm struggling and frustrated, then I need to go back and go over the truth of God's Word again, and renew my mind to that truth. (Romans 12:2.)

We don't want to confuse this with conviction (*not* condemnation) over certain things that need to be corrected. *Conviction* is that uncomfortable feeling when we start to get away from what's right. We need that to keep us on the right track. Understand that when you initially receive Jesus in your life, all past sins and wrong doings are completely wiped away. You don't have to go back and try to confess each one. They're gone and forgotten. Our focus needs to be on today. In the process of our growth in Christ, we will miss it at times. The Holy Spirit will show us when that happens through conviction.

When conviction comes, all we have to do is admit what we did wrong, receive God's forgiveness, forgive ourselves and make the adjustments. Repent (turn away from what you're not feeling right about) and do what you know is right (with God's help and ability in you), and then continue to walk in freedom. Always going forward, never looking back.

Now, although no amount of good works could have saved us, we do have responsibilities and good works to perform. Ephesians 2:10 tells us that we were created for good works in Christ and explains what that means: "For we are His workmanship, created in Christ Jesus for good works, which God prepared beforehand that we should walk in them."

These works will not make a difference on your value to God or His love for you. They will not make a difference on how you measure up. Good works not only should come from our personal relationship with Jesus but from our gratitude for what's already been done for us by Him. Then it becomes more of a joy, rather than a required job.

It's like the difference of trying to do things for people to hopefully gain their approval and doing things for people out of appreciation because you know they already approve of you. The first is stressful, and the second is easy.

It's through knowing our God that we're able to grab ahold of what we need not only to live, but to live godly. His precious Word is what enables us to walk in a new nature, the divine nature. Knowing Him and His Word is what helps us not to give in to the old corrupted nature. You get to know Him by spending time with Him, praying (which is simply talking to Him), and reading His Word. (2 Peter 1:3–4.)

## True Freedom

2 Peter 1:5–10 KJV

5 And beside this, giving all diligence, add to your faith virtue; and to virtue knowledge;

6 And to knowledge temperance; and to temperance patience; and to patience godliness;

7 and to godliness brotherly kindness; and to brotherly kindness charity.

8 **For if these things be in you, and abound, they make you that ye shall neither be barren nor unfruitful in the knowledge of our Lord Jesus Christ.**

9 **But he that lacketh these things is blind, and cannot see afar off, and hath forgotten that he was purged from his old sins.**

10 **Wherefore the rather, brethren, give diligence to make your calling and election sure: for if ye do these things, ye shall never fall.**

As you start to believe God and His Word, there are some things He wants you to add to your faith. Notice, however, if you're not displaying these godly traits, it just means you forgot where and how it all started. You've lost your focus. Other things have blocked your view. Usually, the main thing is self. If these godly traits aren't flowing in your character, then it's time to go back to the cross, go back to when you were rescued, and consider where you would be if you hadn't been rescued. It not only helps with humility, but also keeps your heart full of gratitude.

When you've been given a gift, and you know that great expense and sacrifice went into it, you will automatically display these kinds of traits at the time of receiving it. And even more so when you know you haven't especially been very good to that person from whom you received it. When we remind ourselves continually of the greatness of God's mercy, which rescued us and pulled us out of such darkness, realizing that we weren't even treating Him right, these characteristics in verses 5 through 7—faith, virtue, knowledge, temperance (self-control), patience, godliness, brotherly kindness, and charity (love)— will become our expression of gratitude, as long as we allow no guilt.

When you walk and live with this frame of mind, you can't go wrong. You will continue getting to know the Lord in a greater way. As you do, God will continue to "work in [you] through Jesus Christ to do what is pleasing to him" (Hebrews 13:21 GW).

Be aware, though, that some people will actually try to put you in bondage, either because they are critical and judgmental, or they are in bondage themselves and are jealous of your freedom. We just have to do as Paul did—don't give them the time of day. Just stay away.

Galatians 2:4–5,16 KJV

4 That because of false brethren unawares brought in, who came in privily to spy out our liberty which we have in Christ Jesus, that they might bring us into bondage:

5 To whom we gave place by subjection, no, not for an hour; that the truth of the gospel might continue with you . . .

16 Knowing that a man is not justified by the works of the law, but by the faith of Jesus Christ, even we have believed in Jesus Christ, that we might be justified by the faith of Christ, and not by the works of the law: for by the works of the law shall no flesh be justified.

Colossians 1:21–23

21 And you, who once were alienated and enemies in your mind by wicked works, yet now He [Jesus] has reconciled

22 in the body of His flesh through death, to present you holy, and blameless, and above reproach in His sight—

23 if indeed you continue in the faith, grounded and steadfast, and are not moved away from the hope of the gospel which you heard, which was preached to every creature under heaven, of which I, Paul, became a minister.

We've got to stay firm in our faith in what Jesus has done for us. It's not according to our perfect performance; it's according to our faith. Yet, that is not a license to do whatever we feel like doing.

We want to do well and obey God's Word because He has been so good to us. Remember, 1 John 4:19 says, "We love him because he *first* loved us."

As God's love demonstrated such sacrifice and selflessness, our love should display the same attitude in our choices we make in life.

**1 Corinthians 6:12** MSG

12 Just because something is technically legal doesn't mean that it's spiritually appropriate. If I went around doing whatever I thought I could get by with, I'd be a slave to my whims.

**1 Corinthians 10:23,24** MSG

23 Looking at it one way, you could say, "Anything goes. Because of God's immense generosity and grace, we don't have to dissect and scrutinize every action to see if it will pass muster."

24 But the point is not to just get by. We want to live well, but our foremost efforts should be to help others live well.

**1 Corinthians 10:23,24**

23 All things are lawful for me, but not all things are helpful; all things are lawful for me, but not all things edify.

24 Let no one seek his own, but each one the other's well-being.

While you're enjoying your freedom, remember to keep *all things* in balance. Don't let yourself get out of control with your freedom. Some people who choose to yield to their flesh might think they're operating in freedom, but in reality they have become a slave to their flesh. What's really freeing is when you have dominance over your flesh.

Keep in mind what you're free from and what you're free to do. Galatians 5:13 says, "For you, brethren, have been called to liberty; only do not use liberty as an opportunity for the flesh, but through love serve one another." We're free to serve. We're not *made* to serve; we *choose* to serve. And that is a privilege!

### 1 Corinthians 10:31,33

**31  Therefore, whether you eat or drink, or whatever you do, do all to the glory of God . . .**

**33  Just as I also please all men in all things, not seeking my own profit, but the profit of many, that they may be saved.**

Paul literally displayed this action just a few books before, in Acts 16. He and Silas were whipped and thrown in prison for telling people about Jesus, and the jailer was given a high charge to keep them secure. But as they were praying and singing praises to God, an earthquake took place and their chains fell off and the doors were opened. They were free to go. When the jailer saw this, he pulled out his sword to kill himself because he knew he would be tormented and put to death by his leaders for letting these prisoners escape. But Paul said loudly, "Do yourself no harm, for we are all here" (v. 28).

The jailer was so touched by this act of love that he ran in and asked Paul what he must do to be saved. And that night he and all his family received Jesus as their Lord. The jailer then washed their stripes, brought them into his house, and fed them. The very next day the authorities released them. This is such an incredible example of what we're talking about.

True freedom is experienced in a selfless lifestyle, with the number one motive to glorify God and help others move forward and find their place in Him.

# CHAPTER 6

∽

# Walking in Newness of Life

Are you beginning to see how great it is to be on the winning side? We live with a new nature now—God's nature. That's what we follow. To really win, however, and stay on top, we've got to die in the sense of putting to death carnality, of every day crucifying our fleshly nature and selfish ambitions. (Colossians 3:5–8.) We "present our bodies a living sacrifice . . ." not conforming to this world. (Romans 12:1–2.) That is the essence of this flesh and spirit battle.

Our carnal, flesh nature wants to do the opposite of what God wants. When the attitudes and thoughts of the flesh arise, instead of just trying to ignore them, we need to see those things nailed to the cross. That way, there's no choice available to give in to them. The apostle Paul explained it this way:

**Galatians 2:19,20**

19 For I through the law died to the law that I might live to God. I have been crucified with Christ; it is no longer

20 I who live, but Christ lives in me; and the life which I now live in the flesh I live by faith in the Son of God, Who loved me and gave Himself for me.

**2 Corinthians 5:15**

15 [Jesus] died for all, that those who live should live no
longer for themselves, but for Him who died for them and
rose again.

To live for Jesus involves constantly putting our flesh under.
It's not a one-time thing. We always have to put to death certain
emotions, wrong thinking, wrong actions, and wrong desires
that come from our carnal nature. Brush it off the same way you
would brush off a fly, by being quick about it and intolerant of
it. As you do, the life and character of Jesus will be seen in you.

**Colossians 3:1–5**

1 If then you were raised with Christ, seek those things which
are above, where Christ is, sitting at the right hand of God.

2 Set your mind on things above, not on things on the earth.

3 For you died, and your life is hidden with Christ in God.

4 When Christ who is our life appears, then you also will
appear with Him in glory.

5 Therefore put to death your members which are on the
earth: fornication, uncleanness, passion, evil desire, and
covetousness, which is idolatry.

**Romans 8:10**

10 If Christ be in you, the body is dead because of sin; but the
Spirit is life because of righteousness.

Since the body (or flesh) is connected to sin, once Christ moves
in, you're body has to be denied certain things it wants. That's
why the scripture says it's dead. And the truth is, that's when *you*
really start to live—abundantly! Our spirit is quickened (made
alive), because we have been put in right standing with God.

**Romans 8:11–13** KJV

11 But if the Spirit of him that raised up Jesus from the dead
   dwell in you, he that raised up Christ from the dead shall
   also quicken your mortal bodies by his Spirit that dwelleth
   in you.

12 Therefore, brethren, we are debtors, not to the flesh, to
   live after the flesh.

13 For if ye live after the flesh, ye shall die: but if ye through
   the Spirit do mortify the deeds of the body, ye shall live.

Notice the important key here: you do this *through* the Spirit.
So, when you're faced with the temptation of the flesh, look to
the Lord for help—draw your attention to Him by beginning to
pray in the Spirit (we'll discuss that more later on), quote the
Word, and worship Him. This will help you adjust your focus.

Peter had to adjust his focus when he faced the temptation
to be fearful during a terrible storm. He and the other disciples
were in a boat fighting to stay afloat when Jesus came walking
on the water towards them. When Peter said, "If it's really You,
Jesus, tell me to come," Jesus told him "Come." Peter stepped
out of the boat and walked on the water but lost his focus on
Jesus by looking at the huge waves. He panicked and began
to sink. Immediately he cried out a simple three-word prayer:
"Lord, save me!" and Jesus did. (Matthew 14:24–32.)

It's not wrong to feel fear; it's just important that we deal
with it and don't give into it or anything else that makes us lose
our focus on Jesus. He told us, "Watch and pray, that ye enter
not into temptation: the spirit indeed is willing, but the flesh is
weak" (Matthew 26:41 KJV). Another time Jesus said, "It is the
Spirit who gives life; the flesh profits nothing. The words that
I speak to you are spirit, and they are life" (John 6:63). It's all
about staying Spirit-minded, not flesh-minded.

So, temptation can come from looking at circumstances or lusting after the wrong things instead of staying focused on Jesus.

**James 1:14,15 KJV**

14 Every man is tempted, when he is drawn away of his own lust, and enticed.

15 Then when lust hath conceived, it bringeth forth sin: and sin, when it is finished, bringeth forth death.

Lust comes from our flesh, and that is why we have to crucify the flesh. Not our physical bodies, but our natural, ungodly desires. We need our physical bodies to accomplish God's purpose here on earth. Therefore, when you're tempted, you need to refuse it that instant. Remember that Jesus is right there ready to help, just as He was when Peter began to sink in the sea.

## A Way of Escape

When we immediately resist the temptation, overcoming it becomes much easier, as we're choosing to depend on God's grace. If we think or dwell on the temptation or toy with it, then we're choosing to handle it on our own, pushing God's grace aside. Jesus said that He'll never leave us or forsake us (Hebrews 13:5), and He will always make a way of escape for us—but it's our choice whether or not we take that way.

**1 Corinthians 10:13**

13 No temptation has overtaken you except such as is common to man; but God is faithful, who will not allow you to be tempted beyond what you are able, but with the temptation will also make the way of escape, that you may be able to bear it.

We can never say, "It's too much for me, I can't handle it." All it takes is looking for and taking the escape route provided. When you take that step, you will find the strength you need to overcome. There's always a way out. The flesh tries to draw you to the temptation, but the Holy Spirit will lead you away from it. Have you ever been faced with a temptation and all of a sudden the scripture that deals with it starts coming to mind? That's our main way of escape. We take it by grabbing ahold of, speaking out, and obeying those scriptures.

Verse 13 also shows us that we are not alone. We all face temptations. That's why we need to help each other and stick together. There is strength in numbers. This is the reason the enemy wants to isolate us and make us feel we are alone in whatever we're going through, and that no one would understand. Not only can we relate to each other, but even better, the Lord can relate to us. He's been through temptation and overcome it, so He knows exactly how to help us.

This escape plan is how Jesus dealt with His time of temptation. (Matthew 4:1–11.) We'll talk more on this later, but Satan tempted Jesus in the wilderness, hoping He would turn away from His faith in God. That's the enemy's purpose for us too. Jesus took the way of escape we're talking about here—with the Word—and so can we.

Hebrews 2:18 tells us, "For in that [Jesus] Himself has suffered, being tempted, He is able to aid those who are tempted." He feels the pain and understands that it can be tough, but He wants to show us just how much tougher we can be because His Spirit dwells in us. And because of that we know that if He overcame it, we can too! It's only by His strength within us.

Genesis 4:7 says "Sin lies at the door. And its desire is for you, but you should rule over it." God said this to Adam and Eve's son, Cain, when Cain got angry and his countenance dropped because his brother Abel's offering was accepted by God over his. Abel had given his first and best to God; Cain didn't. God gave Cain a warning and a way out, but instead of making a correction in his attitude and learning a lesson, Cain chose not to take that way out. He gave in to the sin and killed his brother. (v. 8.) Sin causes us to do things we don't want to do, if we let it.

Paul tells us in Romans 6:14, "Sin shall not have dominion over you." We have to get a grip on this truth that sin cannot control us. We have been given the authority to dominate over sin.

### Romans 6:11–13 NLT

11 So you also should consider yourselves to be dead to the power of sin and alive to God through Christ Jesus.

12 Do not let sin control the way you live; do not give in to sinful desires.

13 Do not let any part of your body become an instrument of evil to serve sin. Instead, give yourselves completely to God, for you were dead, but now you have new life. So use your whole body as an instrument to do what is right for the glory of God.

When sin presents itself to you, envision yourself as dead to it. A dead man cannot be tempted. Then see yourself rich in more than just material ways, fully alive in God and enjoying the blessings and benefits He has loaded you with, and allowing everything about you to operate in righteousness. (Psalm 68:19.) The ways of the flesh are dead to us. We now walk in the newness of the life we've been given in Jesus Christ.

# CHAPTER 7

# It's All by Grace and Faith

There's not one person who can't relate to the wrestling match between flesh and spirit. Even if someone seems to have a better handle on controlling their flesh, they had to get to that place. Or maybe their issues are not as evident. Is there such a thing as a garden that has never had weeds show up? Not on this earth.

What our flesh has had the freedom to do in our past is a factor. As born-again Christians we have the power to resist those things and stay steady in our commitment to walking in the Spirit, but the way we were brought up can make a difference on the extent of the battle.

The flesh nature is very evident in toddlers. They often openly test their boundaries. You tell them not to do something and they suddenly want to do it even more. In fact, they will do it—until they learn it's not worth the consequences you give them. If you will discipline them consistently, they will know how to be more self-disciplined as adults. It will make it easier for them to not let their flesh run their lives. If you had a tough or undisciplined background that has caused you to have more struggles in certain areas in the flesh, be assured that you can overcome them. Still, you must not allow yourself to excuse yourself.

By the grace of God and your choices you make today, your whole situation can be turned around. Eventually people will think you had the perfect home life by the fruits they see in you. When you meet someone who is in great shape, and they tell you they had lost 100 pounds or so, it's usually hard to believe. That's what God can do for you in helping you control your carnal nature—and much more than you can imagine!

No matter what kind of upbringing we've had, as long as we're in this earthly body, regardless of who we are, it has to be "tilled." Weeds of ungodly thoughts, choices, and behavior have to be pulled; flesh has to be refused daily.

Just as the devil made the forbidden tree in the garden seem so much better to Eve than all the others, he approaches us the same subtle, enticing way, trying to get us to desire the very things we can't or shouldn't have, the very things that will destroy us. Because of Eve giving in to the devil's temptation, giving in is now part of the flesh nature. This nature actually began in Satan when he wanted something he couldn't have—God's position. (See Isaiah 14:12–15.) It's no surprise that it ended badly for him.

The apostle Paul talks candidly about this battle between the flesh and the Spirit.

### Romans 7:15–25

15 For what I am doing, I do not understand. For what I will to do, that I do not practice; but what I hate, that I do.

16 If, then, I do what I will not to do, I agree with the law that it is good.

17 But now, it is no longer I who do it, but sin that dwells in me.

18 For I know that in me (that is, in my flesh) nothing good dwells; for to will is present with me, but how to perform what is good I do not find.

19 For the good that I will to do, I do not do; but the evil I will not to do, that I practice.

20 Now if I do what I will not to do, it is no longer I who do it, but sin that dwells in me.

21 I find then a law, that evil is present with me, the one who wills to do good.

22 For I delight in the law of God according to the inward man.

23 But I see another law in my members, warring against the law of my mind, and bringing me into captivity to the law of sin which is in my members.

24 O wretched man that I am! Who will deliver me from this body of death?

25 I thank God—through Jesus Christ our Lord! So then, with the mind I myself serve the law of God, but with the flesh the law of sin.

Remember, the mind is part of the soul, which has been given to us to make choices. That's what we use to decide which we're going to heed to, the spirit or the flesh. We've seen that God told us through Paul to renew our minds because it's transforming. (Romans 12:2.) We do that with the Word of God.

Jesus is the Word that "became a human being and . . . lived among us" (John 1:14 CEV). When you learn "the truth that comes from him," you can "throw off your old sinful nature and your former way of life, which is corrupted by lust and deception," and "instead, let the Spirit renew your thoughts and attitudes" (Ephesians 4:21–23 NLT). In other words, the Word tells you what's right to do and the Holy Spirit enables you to do it.

When you know what's right to do, the flesh pulls really hard to try to stop you from doing it. And when you know what you shouldn't do, the flesh pulls hard to get you to do it because it's sinful, and sin can seem pleasurable "for a season" (Hebrews 11:25 KJV). The flesh is an enemy of the Spirit. It will especially try to stop you from drawing closer to God and building up your spirit.

The Romans 7 passage (above) describes this struggle, making it sound as if Paul's in a losing battle. But the last verse in that passage sounds like he's got the victory. How's that? He got the revelation, and it's in the very next chapter:

Romans 8:1–5

1 There is therefore now no condemnation to those who are in Christ Jesus, who do not walk according to the flesh, but according to the Spirit.

2 For the law of the Spirit of life in Christ Jesus has made me free from the law of sin and death.

3 For what the law could not do in that it was weak through the flesh, God did by sending His own Son in the likeness of sinful flesh, on account of sin: He condemned sin in the flesh,

4 that the righteous requirement of the law might be fulfilled in us who do not walk according to the flesh but according to the Spirit.

5 For those who live according to the flesh set their minds on the things of the flesh, but those who live according to the Spirit, the things of the Spirit.

So, you need to determine what you're after and go after it with all your might!

Romans 8:6–9

6 For to be carnally minded is death, but to be spiritually minded is life and peace.

7 Because the carnal mind is enmity against God; for it is not subject to the law of God, nor indeed can be.

8 So then, those who are in the flesh cannot please God.

**9 But you are not in the flesh but in the Spirit, if indeed the Spirit of God dwells in you. Now if anyone does not have the Spirit of Christ, he is not His.**

Because of the Spirit of the Lord now dwelling in us, we have the ability to walk in the Spirit and not give in to the pressure of the flesh. The essence of these two chapters is that Romans 7 explains the issues we deal with and Romans 8 gives the solution. It boils down to how we choose to walk.

## Get Tuned In

As we are going forward, we have two routes to choose from: the way of the flesh or the way of the Spirit. It takes faith to walk (or live) in the Spirit and not in the flesh. (Galatians 5:25.) You've got to believe that you can do it (because you can!), and that it's worth it (because it is!). The things that your natural, earthly body wants are contrary to, or against, the Spirit (Galatians 5:17), but with God's help you can crucify "the flesh with the affections and lusts" (v. 24 KJV).

I know at times this battle can seem pretty complicated. You might be thinking that it would have been nice if it was a little simpler, but I believe that the whole point of this being such a mystery is to push people to seek the Lord. If it was so simple in the natural, then who would seek Him? Searching to understand God's ways draws us closer to Him. How intelligent is that?

Jeremiah 33:3 says, "Call to Me, and I will answer you, and show you great and mighty things, which you do not know." Notice that the more quality time you spend with the Lord, the more you understand and the more clearly you see things. But when you slack in your time with the Lord, things are kind of foggy again. It comes and goes just like that. When you're tuned in, it's simple. When you're not, it's complicated.

Here's the bottom line: The devil will try to deceive you with temptations to sin, as he did Eve in the garden, to draw you away from God. Nevertheless, Christians who are really serious about walking with the Lord (or having a relationship with Him), whose actions and faith in God's Word reveal it, can have access to the true answers and understand "the simplicity that is in Christ" (2 Corinthians 11:3).

If you're at a place where everything seems foggy, just know that it doesn't have to take long to clear it all up again. Some people get into a mind-set where they believe they've let things go for too long and they feel overwhelmed, thinking that it's going to take a lot to get them cleared up again and back to where they were. In the natural it can be like that with finances, weight, health, and other life issues. Many people want to start but easily give up because the results they desire seem so far off. Of course, waiting only pushes them further back. However, to get things fixed in the Spirit realm, it really doesn't have to take long at all.

The enemy wants to deceive you into thinking that it works like the natural realm (where change often takes a long time) so he can keep you in that slump. The truth is it's all by the grace (unearned favor) of God and by faith in His Word. Once you catch on to that fact and get into a steady, close walk with the Lord, you will find the motivation to tackle the natural things you want to achieve. As you're growing in the Spirit, you'll see that the natural things will begin changing quicker than normal.

Third John 1:2 says, "Beloved, I wish above all things that thou mayest prosper and be in health, even as thy soul prospereth" (KJV). As your soul prospers by allowing the Spirit to control it, you will see the natural things follow right behind.

# CHAPTER 8

# Making Choices, Taking Action

Following the Spirit on the inside of you leads to love, joy, peace, patience, kindness, goodness, faithfulness, gentleness (meekness, humility), and self-control. These are called the *fruits of the Spirit* in Galatians 5:22–23, and they are the opposite of what arises in your flesh. When you decide to react in the opposite way of what your flesh wants, it's like sprinkling weed killer on your "ground."

Verse 16 talks about following the Spirit, saying, "This I say then, Walk in the Spirit, and ye shall not fulfill the lust of the flesh" (KJV), yet so often people try to do this backwards. They try on their own to stop having certain attitudes or behaviors of the flesh, and they only get frustrated and disappointed. If, instead, we would focus on purposely allowing the Spirit to govern us and acting out the fruits of the Spirit that following Him produces, we wouldn't do what the flesh wants. You can't do both.

It's like Adam and Eve having the choice of the two trees in front of them—the one that was okay for them to eat from and the one that was not. (Genesis 3.) The enemy will do his best to lure you to what's not okay, as he did to Eve, who then drew Adam into the deception. If they had gone directly towards the right tree, they would have been able to enjoy it, not even thinking about the forbidden one. To just stand looking at the tree they were not suppose to eat from, trying to resist eating from it, did not work. You've got to press towards the right choice, and keep your attention on that.

It's about practicing the fruits of the Spirit. Focus on what you should be doing instead of what you should not be doing. When you're tempted to act out in the flesh, first of all say, "No, I won't allow that!" Then make yourself act out in one of the spiritual fruits (of Galatians 5), opposite of what you feel. Remember that you have the power of God on the inside to help you, once you are born again. Just keep your focus on Jesus and what His Word says.

Let's look at some various temptations of the flesh and ways we can resist them by our reaction to them. These reactions are basically examples of walking in the Spirit.

*Anger.*

Are you tempted to act out in anger? Quickly respond with gentleness. You won't feel like it at the moment, but it can suppress that anger. The Word of God cannot fail. If you walk in the Spirit (such as gentleness), then you will not fulfill the lust of the flesh (such as anger). You can count on it really working.

The best way to help you respond in gentleness is to follow the principle found in James 1:19, "Let every man be swift to hear, slow to speak, slow to wrath." Don't be in a hurry to react, but do be in a hurry to listen to what your conscience is saying. Pay close attention to what you hear or see that's getting you stirred up. Think about where those words or actions really came from and who inspired them. Then take a moment to consider how you want to react; what kind of words and emotion do you really want to use. That popular phrase "Count to ten" to help you cool off, definitely has truth to it. If you have to walk away, do so.

*Jealousy and Envy.*

Another form of temptation that may plague you is being tempted to be jealous or envious of someone. In that case, set your heart to appreciate and enjoy that individual's unique gifts, knowing they came from God to bless people. Pray for the person's character to grow with his or her gifts, in the same way that you would want to be prayed for.

*Aggravation and Bitterness.*

Perhaps you're tempted to be aggravated or bitter towards someone because your personalities clash, or maybe they did something to offend you. Instead, set your heart to be patient and see their needs or insecurities, and especially, forgive them. It's a choice. Say it out loud every time the offense comes to mind. The feelings may not change the first time or two that you say you choose to forgive, but they definitely will if you stick with it. Keep in mind that only people who are hurting dish out hurt on others. Pray for them and reach out with kindness. Consider your own needs and insecurities and how you want others to understand and be patient with you.

*Selfishness.*

If you're tempted to wallow in self-pity, choose joy. It's in you, as well. You've just got to stir it up. And if you're tempted to be consumed with selfish desires, just turn your focus outward and start giving your time, attention, finances, and so on, to others.

## Putting God Second.

If you're tempted to put something before God, deny some time or attention to whatever it is, and replace it with time with God or doing some sort of service for the kingdom.

## Sexual Immorality.

Being tempted to commit adultery is probably more prevalent in today's society than ever before. If you struggle with this temptation, use self-control (you can't say you don't have self-control because Galatians 5:23 says it's one of the fruits of the Spirit that is in you) and consider love for your spouse and for all the ones involved that would be badly affected. Love is not a feeling; it's an action and a commitment. (See 1 Corinthians 13:4–8.) And especially stay away from anything that generates temptation and places where something could happen, even in your mind. Remember that sticking around and dwelling on the temptation is what got Eve in trouble.

If you make sure your commitment is to God first (as it should be), then because you know that He is always aware of what you're doing, you can do what's right. Even if it seems you have an excuse such as feeling neglected—your spouse is not meeting your needs, so he/she doesn't deserve your faithfulness—just consider that God does deserve it and you know how He feels about adultery.

That goes for fornication (sexual relations before marriage) as well. Remember longsuffering or patience. The love and respect you have for God, the other person, and yourself, determine that you will wait until marriage. Realize that to do so, you must set boundaries.

The first part of 1 Corinthians 6:18 says to flee sexual immorality. So, although some temptations you meet head on and simply correct with the Word of God, adultery and fornication are ones that you have to physically run from (or quickly get away from) as well as speak the Word. That way you're reminding yourself why you are running. Joseph in the Old Testament showed the perfect example of this.

Genesis 39:7–12

7 And it came to pass after these things that his master's wife cast longing eyes on Joseph, and she said, "Lie with me."

8 But he refused and said to his master's wife, "Look, my master does not know what is with me in the house, and he has committed all that he has to my hand.

9 There is no one greater in this house than I, nor has he kept back anything from me but you, because you are his wife. How then can I do this great wickedness, and sin against God?"

10 So it was, as she spoke to Joseph day by day, that he did not heed her, to lie with her or to be with her.

11 But it happened about this time, when Joseph went into the house to do his work, and none of the men of the house was inside,

12 that she caught him by his garment, saying, "Lie with me." But he left his garment in her hand, and fled and ran outside.

First, Joseph gave his reason why he could not do such a thing. His reason was not because of what Potiphar had done for him and entrusted him with, but he recognized that his position was God's doing. He said, "How then can I do this . . .

against God?" Wanting to do right before God was the strength of his motive. And though she hounded him every day, he did not take the time to listen or entertain what she was asking. So, we can see that he did his part by avoiding her request, and then he literally ran from her.

*Strife.*

If you're tempted to be in strife, challenge yourself to do all you can to make peace. Romans 12:18 says, "If it is possible, as much as depends on you, live peaceably with all men." Pride (which is in the flesh) always has to have the last word, and is determined to prove it's right. So, the right approach to this would be to hold our tongue, or answer peacefully. It's scriptural: "A soft answer turns away wrath, but a harsh word stirs up anger" (Proverbs 15:1.)

*Alcohol and Drugs.*

If you're tempted to go drink your troubles away or escape them through drugs, choose to get in the presence of God instead, where there's "fullness of joy" (Psalm 16:11); where the heaviness of your troubles really will vanish, and there's no hangover to follow. Not only will the heaviness go away but the process of the deliverance from your troubles will begin. David said in Psalm 34:6 that he cried "and the Lord heard him, and saved him out of all his troubles."

So many people take drugs and get drunk to ease the pain of life and to make them forget about their problems. The truth is it only makes the problems worse. God says not to be drunk because it will destroy our lives, but to be filled with His Spirit instead. (Ephesians 5:18.) What God offers always exceeds what the devil offers by far. God's offers are always for our good. The devil's offers are completely opposite. He makes them seem good, but in reality they are always traps, set up for our destruction.

So, instead of turning to drugs and alcohol, ask the Lord to fill you with His Spirit as you are spending time in His presence. Here's how I encourage you to start off.

**Ephesians 5:19,20 KJV**
19 **Speaking to yourselves in psalms and hymns and spiritual songs, singing and making melody in your heart to the Lord;**
20 **giving thanks always for all things unto God and the Father in the name of our Lord Jesus Christ.**

Spiritual songs are spontaneous songs that come up out of your heart. Instead of talking praise and worship, you're singing it, and the giving thanks part will help you to see that it's not as bad as you think, or as it could be. A counselor once told me to consider that there's always someone who has had it worse. That was very helpful advice.

I believe that if you'll go this way instead of taking the world's way of a temporary, so-called "fix" that narcotics and alcohol can bring you, you'll find that the experience is so much greater! Rather than *destruction*, you'll see a work of *construction* taking place.

## Switching Modes

All these things that I have mentioned will be totally against what you feel like doing, but those feelings will change as you stick with it. You just have to be patient. In the Lord you are strong enough and have the control you need to do it. The big secret is learning to stop in your tracks and listen to your heart before doing anything.

Look at the list of the works of the flesh we discussed earlier in Galatians 5:19 and see which ones you seem to have trouble with. Then look at the fruits of the Spirit in verses 22–23 and pick out the opposites of what you have trouble with in the flesh. Write them down and post those fruits in different places in your house where you'll see them every day, as a help and a reminder to you.

You can't just sit around idle, wrestling in your mind with the temptation that arises in your flesh. You've got to take action. You can't just wait for your feelings or mood to change. You have to take charge and make them change. Don't let your emotions dictate your relationship and commitment to God. The minute you realize you're in the flesh mode, switch to the spirit mode. You can do that in an instant—as long as it takes just to make the decision to do it. Kind of like when family members get into strife about something, and then a well-respected guest shows up. It's amazing how quickly the attitudes can change. You've got to start by recognizing what you're dwelling on. If it's something negative, or something that's arousing your flesh, begin to quote scripture. That will help redirect your thoughts and attention.

*God's Word* is the perfect mood changer and attitude adjuster. That's the first step in switching modes. Then begin to glorify God and *give Him thanks* for all His goodness. And be sure *to pray in the Spirit.* Just as we are quick to take medicine for physical pain, we need to do these things quickly, when needed, with the same confidence we put in the medication.

Don't be deceived into thinking that you can't help yourself. When you finally realize that you really can, you will experience true victory and step into a whole new level in your walk with God!

## Soul Control

Going to a new level is fueled by our choices. By choice, we can control our soul (our will, our emotions, and what we keep our minds on). For example, our *will* is either going to do what the flesh wants, or what the spirit wants. Our *emotions* will cry out in self-pity, express anger and other negative feelings (which lean to the flesh), or our emotions will cry out with overwhelming gratitude, express joy and excitement and other positive feelings (which lean to the spirit). Our *minds* will think negatively, immorally, or doubtfully (which is fleshly), or our minds will think faithfully, positively, purely, or unselfishly (which is spiritual).

In the first two verses in Psalm 103, David is telling his soul to bless the Lord with everything in him, and to not forget all of God's benefits. Obviously, his spirit was pulling on his soul. I imagine, on the other hand, that his flesh was trying to make him miserable by looking at certain circumstances and forgetting the benefits that he had in God, trying to discourage him from trusting the Lord. But David made his decision in which direction his soul was going to go.

In Psalm 43:5 David says, "Why art thou cast down, O my soul? and why art thou disquieted within me? hope in God: for I shall yet praise him, who is the health of my countenance, and my God" (KJV). Like David, when our soul begins to feel discouraged, anxious, or worried about something, we've got to say, "What's the deal, soul? You're following after the flesh. It's time to turn your attention to God and hope in Him. He's more than enough. He's proven Himself faithful. I'm determined to continually praise Him. He's the One who can change my countenance from sorrow to joy and peace. He is my God and I will behave like it."

We have to be bold in the same way David was by demanding our soul (mind, will, and emotions) to be Spirit-led. It's our responsibility to choose and to enforce our decision.

Controlling your thought life by speaking the Word (the truth) keeps your mind full of the right things and leaves no room for wrong thinking. It's really hard to think on one thing as you're saying something else. That's one good reason we should say the scriptures out loud. Plus, it increases our faith because "Faith comes by hearing . . . the Word of God" (Romans 10:17).

When a thought comes to you, ask yourself, "Is this something I would be willing to publicly report?" If it's not, than cast the thought out. I'm not saying you have to share every thought. Just make sure they're pure enough that you would if you had to.

The Bible tells us what we should be thinking on:

**Philippians 4:8 KJV**

8 **Finally, brethren, whatsoever things are true, whatsoever things are honest, whatsoever things are just, whatsoever things are pure, whatsoever things are lovely, whatsoever things are of good report; if there be any virtue, and if there be any praise, think on these things.**

Dig and find the scriptures you need to be speaking to correct the thoughts that arise. Write them down and post those around your house as well.

So, first you make the decision and set the goal of what you really want—to follow the Spirit or the flesh. Then you take the steps or actions to make that decision happen. Some things will require more discipline or sacrifice. An example of an action could be if you chose to remain a virgin until your wedding day, then you would have to set up boundaries to make that happen, like avoiding being alone, or being sure to stay in public settings with the opposite sex. Never trust your flesh! Philippians 3:3 says, "Have no confidence in the flesh."

Even the decision of getting to know the Lord more takes steps, and that would be to spend more time with Him and in His Word. This principle can be applied to any circumstance. You've got to find what to do or what not to do to follow through with your decisions.

This really is easier than we think, but it does take effort. The key to accomplishing this is to keep your spirit strong and stirred up (that's where the fruits of the Spirit are—right inside you). It's like a game of tug-a-war. The stronger side always wins! We determine which is stronger in our personal lives. We decide which will dominate!

The best way to make sure your spirit is stronger is by feeding it every day with the Word of God, spending time alone with Him, praying and regularly worshiping Him, and praying in the Spirit. Also, taking time to listen to Him, obeying Him, and staying tuned in to His leading throughout the day. That's walking with the Lord. The closer and more intimately you walk with Him, the more His character will flow through you. As the saying goes, "You are who you hang around with."

# CHAPTER 9

# Powerful Essentials—
# the Word and Prayer

When I was 16 years old, I was sitting in my parents' living room one day, listening to some Christian music of theirs. I began talking to the Lord, saying, "I want so badly to live for You, but why do I keep messing up? How do I be strong?"

Within minutes, words from a song jumped out at me with lyrics about making God's words a part of me and they would make me strong. So, I began to read the Bible two to three times a day, and in the evenings, I would take our dog for a walk and talk to the Lord.

That was one of the most wonderful times of my life. I was amazed at how much stronger and more sensitive to the Lord I was becoming. It was summer, so I didn't have any distractions or peer pressure from school to deal with. It was just God and me!

After about a week, during one of my walks, I strongly sensed the Lord was warning me about something coming up, telling me to be on guard. My response was, "Nothing can take me away from this!" How wrong I was. ("Therefore let him who thinks he stands take heed lest he fall"—1 Corinthians 10:12.)

Shortly after that, a friend from my mom's church came to stay with me for a couple weeks at my dad's. She was not walking with the Lord at all. Finding time to read became less and less, because of her constantly being there. I didn't realize then that it's not about *finding* time, it's about *making* time, and that the devil will always try to bring up things to fill up our time! Well, her influence became too much for me, especially when I started trying to fight it on my own.

I always had the wrong perspective while growing up. I looked to depend on my performance rather than the Lord's performance and how He took my place and did for me what I could never do. So I was very hard on myself. I'm not talking about being self-disciplined, because we definitely need that. I'm talking about my attitude towards myself. I thought that if I messed up I was automatically backslidden. Many times I would stay in that slump until the next revival, and then at the altar call I would get right with God.

I went through a lot of hardships in my childhood, such as my parents divorcing when I was about four; after that, court battles, going back and forth between Mom and Dad, and other, even more devastating things. I always carried guilt and shame, trying so hard to measure up. I remember saying to myself in my early childhood, "I'm going to be a perfect angel today." Of course, that never happened, so the guilt would just build. But, one thing stands out strong and has preserved me. I often sensed the presence of the Lord in my room, starting at a very young age, especially in my darkest moments.

I believe the prayers of my two grandmas have had a lot to do with that. Never underestimate your prayers for your kids, grandkids, or anyone else. Even if you don't have control over the parent's choices, your prayers *will* affect them.

Something I do want to make clear is that although my parents may have made mistakes (just as we all have done), I have the utmost respect for them. After their divorce, as they got back into church, I've watched their devotion to God grow. Their love and commitment to God and to the family has inspired me greatly.

Some of the best influential memories are when I would get up every morning and find my mom sitting in the living room, reading her Bible and devotional. And my dad, sitting in the hallway at night when my brothers and I were little, as we were in our beds with our doors open, and he would read the Bible to us. I lived with my mom more than I did my dad, and whenever I would talk to him on the phone, he would always ask me, "Are you reading your Bible?" I'm so grateful for the sound biblical instruction and advice I have received from them.

By the end of my friend's visit, however, I caved in and was pressured into doing things that were against my convictions. I can't even express how angry and disappointed I was at myself. I know now that mind-set is the trap the enemy uses to defeat us; it has to be shaken off and adjusted immediately. Back then, though, I totally gave up and began to run hard, taking pretty much whatever I was offered.

To me, there was no sense in setting up standards. You're either all the way in or all the way out. My attitude was, "What difference does it make what I do? I'm already on the wrong path." All that would go through my mind was, "How could I, after what Jesus did for me?" I ran from God for two years, sensing the tug of the Holy Spirit at times, trying to get me to turn around. My response was, "I can't . . . I just keep failing . . . I don't want to keep letting You down!" I was in total ignorance, again, having the wrong perspective.

Right after I graduated from high school, I found out that I was pregnant. I had the test done at a clinic where a friend had taken me. As soon as the doctor gave me the results, I started crying, so the doctor immediately took me to their counselor, who tried really hard to talk me into aborting the baby. She said, "It's easy. The procedure will only take five minutes, and you'll be out of the office in an hour, *if* you do it within three months. No one will ever know. You can do it after three months, but it will take longer."

I always did my best to hide everything I was doing wrong from my parents because I didn't want to hurt them, but this time I couldn't. The counselor, with the help of the devil, made this choice they offered me a tempting thought—but that thought didn't stay long. Thank God for the love of children He gave me, and for my parents' and grandmas' effective prayers!

Now, if you have had an abortion, don't feel bad, thinking, "Why didn't He give me that love for children so I wouldn't have done that?" Sin is sin. I've done plenty of other things that maybe you haven't because you were stronger in those areas. The good news is it's all under the blood of Jesus. (1 John 1:7.) And we have to forgive ourselves and forget about it just as He has. (Hebrews 8:12.)

### "You Can Still Come to Me."

After crying myself to sleep night after night, wondering what I was going to do, the presence of the Lord showed up in my room one afternoon. I was sitting at the foot of my bed, facing the wall, realizing that this position was symbolic to where my life was at that moment. It was time to make a choice, and I knew I would be released to follow the path I chose.

Spiritually, I could see the Lord with His arms open on one side, saying, *You can still come to Me.* I told Him that I wanted to raise this child in church. He gave me the understanding that I would have to make the same choice for myself in order for it to truly affect my baby. I said, "I want to, but how?" He spoke in my heart, *You just take the first step, and I'll show you the rest,* and I replied, "Ok."

He also gave me some understanding on commitment. I chose at that moment to commit myself to the Lord and I realized that no matter how many times I fall, I would have to quickly repent, get back up, and stick with that commitment.

Shortly after that experience in my bedroom, my mom's church had started a revival. On the first night, when the evangelist finished his sermon, he gave an invitation for salvation. I sensed that I needed to go up to proclaim publicly my decision for Christ, but I sat there, feeling glued to my seat. I looked up at that altar that I had been to so many times before, feeling the fear of failure again. The next thing I knew, the evangelist was sitting right next to me. Obviously, the Lord let him know that I needed a little help. So, I went up with him and knelt at that altar, making my lifetime commitment to Jesus.

I knew I had to get right in the Word and make a commitment to doing that every day, which definitely takes self-discipline. I learned that the best way to make that happen is to give myself a requirement, such as Bible before breakfast. I didn't usually eat breakfast back then, so I had to find something else. I decided my requirement on myself would be to not fix up my outer self (hair and make-up) until I have fixed up my inner self (my heart), by spending time with God and in His Word. You've just got to consider what is important for you to do or have every day, and choose to read your Bible before you allow that. It's so worth it. I found that God's Word, along with prayer and the Holy Spirit, are very powerful weapons the Lord has given us.

So in the rest of this chapter, we're going to take a closer look at the Word and prayer, and then, in the next chapter talk more about the Holy Spirit, because the enemy is no match against these. They build up our faith, hope, and love, which are essential to have in this life.

## God's Word

The Word of God has scripture to combat anything or any kind of temptation the enemy could bring against you. The way you make it work for you is by finding the right scripture that applies to your life situation, then standing firm in your faith in it and declaring it out loud. When you're facing temptation and God brings scripture to your remembrance (your way of escape), boldly speak it out.

This makes me think of a cute story about my oldest daughter when she was five years old. We were out of town on vacation and my son, who was ten years old, had gotten sick and was in the bathroom throwing up. My daughter went to the door and got down on the floor to talk to him under the door. She said, "Clayton, say what I say. By Jesus' stripes I am healed." He repeated it and was feeling better in no time. It really works—especially when you've got the faith of a child!

Jesus gave us this illustration when Satan came to tempt Him in the wilderness. (Matthew 4:1–11.) We looked at this story earlier, but the point here is that Satan will even try to confuse you by using scripture out of context. That's why it's so important to study and get to know the Word. He tried that with Jesus, but Jesus straightened him out with the right scripture. We can do the same thing.

After a few times of Jesus resisting him with the Word, the devil left and the angels came and ministered to the Lord. That's the perfect example of how to handle the lies and temptation from the enemy. When you handle it that way, your outcome will be the same. You probably won't see angels, but the devil will leave *for a time* (Luke 4:13), and you'll be strengthened and experience refreshment and comfort from the presence of God. Do understand that the devil will leave, but he comes back later with another plan of attack. Every time you defeat him, though, you grow stronger and wiser.

James 1:2–4

2 **My brethren, count it all joy when you fall into various trials,**

3 **knowing that the testing of your faith produces patience.**

4 **But let patience have its perfect work, that you may be perfect and complete, lacking nothing.**

When you're in the middle of a trial or temptation, it's easy to feel overwhelmed with doubt and frustration, as I was. It's easy to wonder if you're really going to make it. But that's when you can get the best workout for your faith—when you've got to reach down, grab ahold of that faith inside you, and believe anyway. It's not about what you feel, it's about what you know and believe. That's why feeding on the Word daily is so vital—it builds your faith.

God's Word is more important to your spirit than food is to your body. Job, who went through a terrible trial and eventually came out victorious, said in Job 23:12, "I have esteemed the words of His mouth more than my necessary food" (KJV).

For new believers especially, starting in the New Testament is essential because that's the new covenant in which we live. I'm certainly not taking away from the Old Testament. The Old Testament contains information on the old covenant that people lived under before Jesus came to this earth. It has great examples and reveals to us how we got to where we are.

Some Old Testament books are Proverbs, which is full of wisdom that most definitely needs to be applied to our lives, and Psalms, which is full of David's prayers and songs to the Lord. And although David talked about people being his enemies, the New Testament makes it clear that we don't fight against people. The devil is our enemy. (See Ephesians 6:11–12.) Other books, such as Isaiah and Jeremiah, have a lot of encouraging scriptures. Reading first in the Old Testament can be challenging for new believers, however. Here's a brief layout of the New Testament, which makes it a little clearer as to why reading this first is best.

The first four books in the New Testament—Matthew, Mark, Luke, and John—are four different accounts on the life of Jesus when He was here on earth. You'll find more detail in some than in others because they're written by different authors, which were His disciples. After that comes the book of Acts, which is how the church began and, basically, how it should be functioning today. The rest of the books are letters to the churches, which include every believer.

Revelation is the last book in the New Testament, and it's all prophecy concerning the end times. That's another one I don't recommend starting with because it, too, can be pretty challenging to understand at first. When you do feel ready to read it, it's good to also have on hand a book about Revelation written by a trusted author who has studied it out and can help explain it.

Reading the Bible book by book is better than just skipping around, picking a verse here and there. It helps you to get the full picture and the right meaning. If you're studying a certain subject, however, with the help of a concordance you can study it out by searching for verses that relate to your topic. Just make sure you have the full understanding by reading what's just before and just after the verse. It's also good to have a pen and paper with you to jot down things you learn and things that God reveals to you.

No matter how many times you read the Bible, you will always learn more. It's a supernatural book. Hebrews 4:12 says, "The word of God is alive and powerful. It is sharper than the sharpest two-edged sword, cutting between soul and spirit, between joint and marrow. It exposes our innermost thoughts and desires" (NLT). The Word will always keep you on the right track if you will hear it and obey it.

Regardless of what you're in the middle of you can be assured that it will soon pass, and as long as you remain in the Word and patient in your faith, you will be amazed at how much stronger your faith will be. Faith pleases God, and it's what we live by. (Hebrews 11:6.) So, that's why we can "count it all joy," as the apostle James said, when we see an opportunity to gain more faith. (James 1:2.) The more you overcome, the more complete, satisfied, and content you are. And according to scripture, "God will bless you, if you don't give up when your faith is being tested. He will reward you with a glorious life, just as He rewards everyone who loves Him" (v. 12 CEV).

Knowing and believing all of this is how you can rejoice in the middle of any circumstance.

## Simple Communication

The Word is an important element of prayer. Prayer is essential because it helps you get the most out of your reading and studying the Bible. And it gets you to a place where you're more focused, open, and sensitive. You receive and understand much more that way. On some occasions you may need to read a couple of verses first to get your mind attentive to the things of God.

Sometimes we complicate our prayers. It should be simple communication from the heart and based on the Word. I have tried to pray in ways that I thought would please God, and I have also just talked to Him as I would a friend. I received much better results with the latter. You've got to approach God believing that you really are talking to Him and that He really is listening. You've got to press in when you don't feel like it, when your natural mind cannot relate to what seems like making believe. In all actuality, you are making yourself believe that this is, in fact, reality. Each individual is choosing to believe something as his or her reality.

Here's another amazing reality in the Word of God that you must believe concerning our sins, which makes all the difference in our prayer life.

**Isaiah 43:25,26**

**25 I, even I, am he who blots out your transgressions for My own sake; and I will not remember your sins.**

26 Put Me in remembrance; let us contend together; state your case, that you may be acquitted [justified].

Isaiah 1:18 KJV

18 Come now, and let us reason together, saith the Lord: though your sins be as scarlet, they shall be as white as snow; though they be red like crimson, they shall be as wool.

God wants you to boldly and confidently approach Him about what His Word says concerning you and your situation. That boldness and confidence come from the realization that your sins are washed away and forgotten. If we truly believe that, then we can believe the rest of His Word.

When talking to God, make sure your praying is not coming from your head or your flesh but from your heart, especially when you are overwhelmed with things that concern you. Crying out to Him in our emotion or flesh will not fix the problem. He certainly cares about what you're going through, and He feels your pain. If you can't help but cry because of the hurt you're experiencing, that's okay—as long as you don't stay in that mode. Flesh does not receive or even want to be involved with spiritual things. It just wants you to feel sorry for yourself, which will get you nowhere. Any time my younger son got hurt when he was a toddler, I would try to comfort (or feel sorry for) him, but he would not receive it. Instead, he would cry out, "Just pray!"

Philippians 4:6,7

6 Be anxious for nothing, but in everything by prayer and supplication, with thanksgiving, let your requests be made known to God;

**7 and the peace of God, which surpasses all understanding, will guard your hearts and minds through Christ Jesus.**

Once you cast your care, you've got to push through and get into faith for the solution and growth you need for your circumstance. The best way to do that is to pray out, and especially thank the Lord for, the scriptures that describe your solutions.

For instance, you can say, "Thank You, Lord, that You are for me and not against me (Romans 8:31); that You're Word says that greater are You who is in me than he that is in the world (1 John 4:4 KJV), and that no weapon formed against me shall prosper (Isaiah 54:17). Thank You for making me more than a conqueror through You who loves me (Romans 8:37). I will not be afraid of bad news; my heart is fixed, trusting in You, Lord (Psalm 112:7 KJV). Thank You, too, that by Your stripes I was and am healed" (1 Peter 2:24; Isaiah 53:5).

Continue to thank God as you take Him at His Word. He wants us to present His Word to Him like that. What actually happens when you start praying the Word of God? Action in the spiritual realm gets stirred up.

**Psalm 103:20 KJV**

**20 Bless the Lord, ye his angels, that excel in strength, that do his commandments, hearkening unto the voice of his word.**

The angels get busy causing God's Word to become reality in your life!

## Getting Started in Prayer

Examples of prayers in the New Testament that are perfect to pray over others and yourself are found in Ephesians

1:17–23, Ephesians 3:14–21, Colossians 1:9–14, and Hebrews 13:20–21. I encourage you to take the time to look them up and use them in your prayer life. I've personally seen great results when consistently praying these.

Remember, praying has to be geared toward your spirit, not your flesh. Trying to pray with your intellect (your mind) can only go so far. Our mind usually just gets in the way, and it certainly can't comprehend what's going on in the Spirit. Be sure you're not just praying to hear yourself and see how long or how good of a prayer you can come up with. (Matthew 6:7.) Sincerely calling out to God from your spirit (the depths of your heart), in faith, is where you will find results and the help you need, and most of all, a genuine relationship with your Father God, through our Lord Jesus Christ.

The best way to start off your praying is with praise and worship, getting all your focus on the Lord and His goodness. Psalm 100:4 says, "Enter into his gates with thanksgiving, and into his courts with praise." That will help your prayer time to be less selfish and more Spirit-led. It gets your eyes on God and His ability instead of just what you need or want. You'll go in the right direction with the right motives.

In Luke 11:2, where Jesus is teaching His disciples how to pray, He starts with "Our Father which art in heaven, hallowed be thy name" (KJV). So, first you recognize who He is and where He is, then you lift up His holy name. Lifting up His name is the same as lifting up His character. You can go on and on about His character. His character is amazing, strong, faithful, merciful, compassionate; it's wisdom, love, consistent, steadfast, peaceful, and so much more.

Something else that can help you get started in prayer is a psalm of praise like "I will be glad and rejoice in You; I will sing praise to Your name, O Most High" (Psalm 9:2). Other praise scriptures will need to be personalized by rewording them to come from you directly to the Lord, as I previously illustrated in praying out your solutions in the Word. Here are a few examples:

- I will sing unto You, Lord. I make a joyful noise to the rock of my salvation. I come before Your presence with thanksgiving, and make a joyful noise unto You with psalms. For Lord, You are the great God, and the great King above all gods. I come to worship and bow down: I will kneel before You, Lord, my maker (Psalm 95:1–3,6);

- I will sing unto You, Lord, as long as I live: I will sing praise to You, my God while I have my being. My meditation of You shall be sweet: I will be glad in You, Lord (Psalm 104:33–34);

- Blessed are You, Lord my strength . . . My goodness, and my fortress; my high tower, and my deliverer; my shield, and You, in whom I trust (Psalm 144:1–2 KJV);

- Everyday will I bless You and I will praise Your name forever and ever. Great are You, Lord, and greatly to be praised; Your greatness is unsearchable (Psalm 145:2–3);

- I make a joyful noise unto You, Lord. I serve You with gladness: I come before Your presence with singing. I know, Lord, that You are God. It is You that has made me, and not me myself; I am yours and I'm a sheep of Your pasture. . . . I'm thankful unto You, and I bless Your name. Lord, You are good; and Your mercy is

everlasting; and Your truth endures to all generations"
(Psalm 100:1–5 KJV).

A perfect illustration of starting this way is found in Acts
4. The chief priests and elders had threatened Peter and John,
and "commanded them not to speak at all nor teach in the
name of Jesus" (v. 18 KJV). They went to the other disciples and
told them about the threats and when they heard it, they, all
together, lifted up their voices and began to pray beginning with
acknowledging who God is and the many things He has created
and done. They focused first on God's power and ability. That
would help cause any problem to shrink.

Notice how unselfish their prayer became. They didn't ask
for deliverance or protection from the threats. They asked for
boldness to speak His Word and for God to stretch forth His
hand to heal, and that signs and wonders would be done in the
name of Jesus. So, instead of becoming fearful, they became
more confident. That is a good indication of how you can know
if you have prayed effectively. After they prayed, the place was
shaken with the power of the Holy Spirit, which filled them,
and their prayer was answered. (vv. 24–31.)

Often our needs and our wants get taken care of as we're
in the middle of worshiping the Lord. Remember the story I
shared about Paul and Silas? They did what I'm talking about
with prayer when they were beaten and then chained up in
prison. In their moment of despair, they chose to pray and sing
praises to God loud enough for all the others in the prison to
hear. Then, all of a sudden, an earthquake struck that not only
opened the doors of the prison, but also broke off their bands.
(Acts 16:22–26.) Don't underestimate what the Lord can do
for you while you're worshiping Him. He says if you delight in
Him, He will give you the desires of your heart. (Psalm 37:4.)

You've also got to be patient. Wait on God, hoping, expecting, and looking eagerly for Him to respond.[2] Sometimes it takes a little time for the flesh to quiet down. Then you can go into the throne room and press on into His presence, to "obtain mercy and find grace to help in time of need" (Hebrews 4:16). It takes humility to get there.

*Receiving* from God what you don't deserve, and *realizing* you did nothing nor could ever do anything to deserve it is humility. You were invited into the throne room because Jesus deserved it for you. It's kind of like getting special seating in a meeting because you are friends with the speaker. You didn't do anything to help your friend prepare or get to the position he or she is in; you're just simply a friend.

As you enter in that way, you can be assured that "God . . . gives grace to the humble" (1 Peter 5:5). We can't do anything without His grace (undeserved favor). It's a supernatural strength and ability to do what you need to do. You can learn so many principles and gain so much wisdom, but the only way you're going to be able to apply it is by grace. So, it's important to realize that in order to rise to the next level the Lord wants to take you to requires humility, which brings an increase of grace.

Once you sense you're in the presence of God, don't just stop, thinking, "Okay, I got there, and I've accomplished my spiritual task." Stay there. That's where you can hear Him better and get clear direction, more grace, and more ability to flow in the anointing (the Holy Spirit) that abides in you. That helps you to be stronger in the Spirit.

# CHAPTER 10

## The Incredible Gift of the Holy Spirit

The Holy Spirit is the third powerful weapon God has given us. He is a special gift sent from the Father to dwell in us to give us strength and comfort, and much more.[3]

God told John, who was baptizing people with water, that the One who he sees the Spirit coming down and landing on is the One who baptizes with the Holy Ghost. He was talking about Jesus when He was here on earth. (John1:33 NLT.) People have thought that when you are born again and receive Jesus in your heart you automatically receive the Holy Spirit. There's definitely a supernatural miracle that takes place inside you. Your spirit is recreated after the character of God. But the actual gift—the baptism or infilling—of the Holy Spirit is an added benefit for us to receive on top of salvation. Acts 19:2–5 reveals this to us:

> [The apostle Paul] said unto them, Have ye received the Holy Ghost since ye believed? And they said unto him, We have not so much as heard whether there be any Holy Ghost. And he said unto them, Unto what then were ye baptized? And they said, Unto John's baptism. Then said Paul, John verily baptized with the baptism of repentance, saying unto the people, that they should believe on him

which should come after him, that is, on Christ Jesus.
When they heard this, they were baptized in the name of
the Lord Jesus. (KJV)

Some individuals also think that the Holy Spirit was only
for back then. Others think that the Holy Spirit is a gift that's
not meant for everyone. However, there are so many scriptures that prove that He's for now and He's for everyone who
believes in Jesus.

Let's start with Luke 11:13:

**"If you then, being evil, know how to give *good gifts* to
your children: how much more will your heavenly Father
give the *Holy Spirit* to those who ask him!"**

"Being evil" here is being natural, clothed in flesh. We all
have messed up and done wrong; we have acted selfishly. We
are imperfect. But God, our Father, is perfect. He not only calls
the Holy Spirit a good gift, but He compares His enthusiasm in
giving Him to anyone who asks, to the way we like giving good
gifts to our own children. We enjoy doing that because we love
them. God enjoys it so much more because He designed it to be
this way, and He *is* love. (1 John 4:8.)

**Acts 10:45 KJV**

**45 They of the circumcision which believed were astonished,
as many as came with Peter, because that on the Gentiles
also was poured out the gift of the Holy Ghost.**

The Israelites are "they of the circumcision" mentioned in
this second verse. The Gentiles are the non-Israelites, the ones
who are not a part of the bloodline of God's chosen people,
according to the old covenant. (Deuteronomy 7:6.) Now,

according to the new covenant, the rest of the world who chooses to receive Christ as their Savior are grafted into this family and can enjoy all the benefits of the Israelites. (Romans 11:17–20 NLT.)

## Heavenly Prayer Language

The Word also shows us that we can receive a heavenly prayer language when we are baptized in the Holy Spirit.

Acts 10:46 KJV

46 They heard them speak with tongues, and magnify God.

Acts 19:6 KJV

6 When Paul had laid his hands upon them, the Holy Ghost came on them; and they spake with tongues, and prophesied.

You may be wondering what it means to speak in tongues and how it is done. Earlier, just before Jesus was taken up to Heaven, after His resurrection, He had told the disciples to "wait for what the Father had promised: the promise you heard from Me" (Acts 1:4 MSG). Jesus further explained to them:

Acts 1:5

5 For John truly baptized with water, but you shall be baptized with the Holy Spirit not many days from now.

So the disciples did what Jesus told them to do and went to a room (called the Upper Room) to wait for the gift of the Holy Spirit to be given to them.

Acts 2:1–4 KJV

1 When the day of Pentecost was fully come, they were all with one accord in one place.

2 And suddenly there came a sound from heaven as of a rushing mighty wind, and it filled all the house where they were sitting.

3 And there appeared unto them cloven tongues like as of fire, and it sat upon each of them.

4 And they were all filled with the Holy Ghost, *and began to speak with other tongues,* as the Spirit gave them utterance.

When you ask for the Holy Spirit, you won't necessarily hear the sound of a rushing mighty wind or see cloven tongues of fire. But as you are praying, you will begin to hear different kinds of words on the inside of you that won't make any sense to you. All you have to do is give voice to them. The more you do, the more it will flow, and you'll be amazed at the difference it makes. Your natural mind may try to interfere by thinking, "This seems really silly," or "That's just me. I didn't really get it." It *is* you speaking it out. But the rest is all Him. Anytime you're having trouble understanding or believing God and His ways, it simply reveals that you are trying to figure it out in the natural. It just doesn't work that way. You've got to get it from your heart (spirit).

### 1 Corinthians 2:14

14 The natural man does not receive the things of the Spirit of God, for they are foolishness to him; nor can he know them, because they are spiritually discerned.

You might start off a little slow and dry, but give it a few minutes. You'll be so glad you did!

Remember that this, too, is done in faith. You have to believe that the words are coming from the Spirit. He'll pray through you to God in a language that you can't understand about specific things that concern you and God's will here on earth.

**1 Corinthians 14:14,15** KJV

**14 If I pray in an unknown tongue, my spirit prayeth, but my understanding is unfruitful.**

**15 What is it then? I will pray with the spirit, and I will pray with the understanding also: I will sing with the spirit, and I will sing with the understanding also.**

When I was around 15 years old, I went up to the altar many times seeking the baptism of the Holy Spirit. I did finally end up speaking a couple of syllables of my prayer language, but it was so frustrating because I made it too complicated. I didn't have to seek for it or *try* to get it; I just had to ask for it and receive it. Just like with salvation. The simple way of salvation is foolish to the world (natural humanity), but once a person receives it there's no convincing him or her that it's not real.

It wasn't until I was in church one day, just praying with the congregation, relaxed, having a heart-to-heart talk with God, that my prayer language began to flow. The mistake I made after that is that I didn't stay consistent with it. This is one thing the devil really wants to keep Christians from doing because he knows you're praying the perfect prayer, and he knows the power you will gain. Plus, he can't understand a word of it.

The bottom line is if it's in the Word, you should believe it no matter how you feel. Just remember that when you got saved, you didn't have to try hard; you just had to confess, believe, and receive. It works the same with being filled with the Holy Spirit and speaking in tongues. I can't express enough how beneficial it is to be consistent, praying every day in the Spirit in our heavenly language and in our own language. The benefits are incomparable.

## Indescribable Benefits

The Holy Spirit is such an incredible gift—the ultimate! He's beyond description. In the list below are some of the benefits of the Holy Spirit, with corresponding scriptures included.

*He gives us power to witness.*

### Acts 1:8

8 **You shall receive power when the Holy Spirit has come upon you; and you shall be witnesses to Me in Jerusalem, and in all Judea and Samaria, and to the end of the earth.**

*He gives us boldness to speak the Word.*

### Acts 4:31

31 **They were all filled with the Holy Spirit, and they spoke the word of God with boldness.**

Peter was a perfect example of this. When Jesus was arrested, Peter followed at a distance, blending with the crowd, to see what was going to happen. But when he was accused of being one of Jesus' followers, he denied it three different times because he was afraid of what would happen to him. After he was filled with the Holy Spirit, however, Peter stood up in front of thousands and not only preached the Word of God, but he also boldly confronted the ones who took part in crucifying Jesus. Then he gave an alter call, telling them to repent and "be baptized in the name of Jesus Christ for the remission of sins" (Acts 2:38). About three thousand souls received Jesus that day. (v. 41.)

*He's our forever Comforter.*

**John 14:16** KJV

16 I will pray the Father, and he shall give you another Comforter, that he may abide with you for ever.

*He is truth and He's with you and in you.*

**John 14:17**

17 The Spirit of truth, whom the world cannot receive, because it neither sees Him nor knows Him; but you know Him, for He dwells with you and will be in you.

*He's your teacher and reminder of God's Word.*

**John 14:26** KJV

26 The Comforter, which is the Holy Ghost, whom the Father will send in my name, he shall teach you all things, and bring all things to your remembrance, whatsoever I have said unto you.

The Holy Spirit will remind you of scripture you've heard or read. That's another good reason why it's so important to read your Bible; it gives Him something to work with.

*He testifies of Jesus.*

**John 15:26** KJV

26 [Jesus said,] "When the Comforter is come, whom I will send unto you from the Father, even the Spirit of truth, which proceedeth from the Father, he shall testify of me."

*He reproves (rebukes, convicts, convinces) the world of sin, righteousness, and judgment.*

**John 16:7,8** KJV

7 [Jesus said,] "Nevertheless I tell you the truth; It is expedient for you that I go away: for if I go not away, the Comforter will not come unto you; but if I depart, I will send him unto you.

8 And when he is come, he will reprove the world of sin, and of righteousness, and of judgment."

*He leads us into truth (which guards us from lying, deceitful paths) and shows us things that are ahead that are going to happen.*

**John 16:13** KJV

13 [Jesus said,] "Howbeit when he, the Spirit of truth, is come, he will guide you into all truth: for he shall not speak of himself; but whatsoever he shall hear, that shall he speak: and he will show you things to come."

There are times that the path ahead may not be made clear, but He will prepare us for what's ahead. For example, I used to drink coffee every day. I didn't even attempt to function until I had my morning cup. Then one day I was impressed to fast coffee for a week. That was extremely hard, but it definitely was a good exercise for my willpower over my flesh. Not long after that, I sensed that I was supposed to quit drinking coffee on a regular basis. It's so neat how the Holy Spirit will meet you where you are and work with you to get you where you need to be. Quitting cold turkey would have been overwhelming, but after realizing I could make it a week without it, I knew I could live without it.

Years later I was diagnosed with a bicuspid aortic valve. It's a condition you're born with. The doctor said that I would eventually have to have a valve transplant. He assured me, though, that my heart looked really good and that it will be a long time before it has to happen. I was amazed by what he said next: drinking energy drinks and too much coffee are the worst things I could do. So, the Holy Spirit led me in a direction to better my health before I even understood why. I just had to trust and obey.

*He glorifies Jesus. He receives from Him and shows it to us.*

**John 16:14**

**14** [Jesus said,] "He will glorify Me, for He will take of what is Mine and declare it to you."

*He gives us the right words to speak when we're put on the spot, or when we have to speak up in the defense of our faith in Jesus.*

**Mark 13:11**

**11** [Jesus said,] "When they arrest you and deliver you up, do not worry beforehand, or premeditate what you will speak. But whatever is given you in that hour, speak that; for it is not you who speak, but the Holy Spirit."

He gives us the words to speak right at the moment we need them. We don't need to worry, scrambling to come up with the right words ahead of time. We just need to trust that He'll come through. The Word says He does, and He does not lie. (See Luke 12:11–12.)

*He's God's anointing in us, and He teaches us and makes things clear to us.*

**1 John 2:27**

27 [The apostle John said,] "The anointing which you have received from [Jesus] abides in you, and you do not need that anyone teach you; but as the same anointing teaches you concerning all things, and is true, and is not a lie, and just as it has taught you, you will abide in Him."

This doesn't mean that you shouldn't listen to godly teaching, because the anointing flows through people *for* you as well. But the Holy Ghost on the inside of you will bear witness whether it's right teaching or not. He'll bring up scripture that it lines up with or that it's contradicting. If it's not agreeing with the Word, don't receive it!

*He helps us give thanks better.*

**1 Corinthians 14:17 tells us that we give thanks well when praying in the Spirit.**

*He helps our infirmities and weaknesses, whatever they are.*

He strengthens us and prays for us, covering things we didn't even know we needed to pray for, detecting and blocking threats (such as danger or opposition within), just like the security program on your computer. And He always prays according to the will of God. He thoroughly searches within. He knows us in and out.

**Romans 8:26,27**

26 Likewise the Spirit also helps in our weaknesses. For we do not know what we should pray for as we ought, but the Spirit Himself makes intercession for us with groanings which cannot be uttered.

27 Now He who searches the hearts knows what the mind of the Spirit is, because He makes intercession for the saints according to the will of God.

*He builds you up on your most holy faith, and He keeps you walking in the love of God.*

Jude 1:20,21

20 But you, beloved, building yourselves up on your most holy faith, praying in the Holy Spirit,

21 keep yourselves in the love of God, looking for the mercy of our Lord Jesus Christ unto eternal life.

*He speaks mysteries, things you don't know about.*

1 Corinthians 14:2 AMP

2 For one who speaks in an unknown tongue does not speak to people but to God; for no one understands him or catches his meaning, but by the Spirit he speaks mysteries [secret truths, hidden things].

*He encourages you and builds you up.*

1 Corinthians 14:4 AMPC

4 He who speaks in a [strange] tongue edifies and improves himself.

*He is **not** a Spirit of fear; He is the Spirit of power, love, and a sound mind.*

2 Timothy 1:6,7

6 Therefore I remind you to *stir up the gift of God* which is in you through the laying on of my hands.

**7 For God has not given us a spirit of fear, but of power and of love and of a sound mind.**

We don't just automatically flow in all these things in the natural. That's why it says you've got to "stir up the gift." Don't neglect the Spirit within you. Let Him pray through you in His heavenly language daily, and throughout each day. Let Him live big in you by using the same steps we've gone over concerning walking in the Spirit and keeping your spirit sensitive to Him and to His leading.

## Stay Tuned In

The Holy Spirit will help you in every detail (big and little) of your life in which you invite Him to help you. He's even got the best diet plan. If you'll stay tuned in to Him, He'll let you know when you've had enough. Just like my coffee experience, He'll let you know things you should or should not be eating or drinking. And He usually does it ever so gently, such as, *Do you really need that?* or *Don't you think you've had enough?* But occasionally He is stern, depending on the urgency of the circumstance. He's like having your own 24/7 personal life trainer/coach. If we'll follow His guidance, we will be perfectly fit and prepared for everything God has planned for us.

# CHAPTER 11

# Happy, Content, and Completely Filled

All of what we've been talking about works the same way as your natural body. If you're not physically fit, you won't do as well in any sport or physical activity, no matter how hard you try. If you're not spiritually fit, you can only go so far as well. You can limit all the abilities God has put inside you (just like muscles are limited when they're not built up).

When you seem to be having more trouble with the flesh, it may be that you're feeding it too much. Of course, I'm not just talking about food here. In your body you have muscle and you have fat. You choose which one you want built up and which one you want less amount of. The same goes for your spirit and flesh.

Cravings of the flesh grow as you feed them—and it just wants more! Do you notice that if you eat something sweet one day, you crave it more the next day? Or if you watch a movie one night, you want to watch another the next night? Habits of the flesh are created quickly. It wants more food, more dessert, more TV, more entertainment!

What you choose to entertain yourself with makes a big difference on how much trouble you have with the flesh. Music and media have a more powerful influence than most people realize. After I got saved and I started growing in my relationship with the Lord, a friend of mine came to my house for a visit. While I was busy doing something she turned my radio on to a secular station, and I realized that I wasn't comfortable with that music anymore. It took me back to memories in the world and familiar feelings that I did not want to be experiencing again. I could feel it really pulling on my flesh. I knew it wouldn't be good for me to allow that in my life. I needed all the help I could get to be totally established in my walk with God.

The devil uses certain kinds of music to lure people away from the Lord and to hinder their relationship with Him in such a deceitful way. He starts with making it fun and seemingly harmless. Of course, almost any temptation he offers is enjoyable to your flesh at first. Remember that the pleasures of sin only last a season. (Hebrews 11:25 KJV.)

Ezekiel 28:13–15 gives a description of how Lucifer (who is now the devil) was created. The last part of verse 13 says, "The workmanship of thy tabrets and of thy pipes was prepared in thee" (KJV). He obviously knows about music and how it works. It's highly influential, which makes it a good reason to be extremely cautious in your listening choices. Be aware, too, that some so-called Christian music does not have a true Christian message. The Christian title is there, but the lyrics are full of natural expressions that go against the truth in God's Word. Overall, there is plenty of inspiring Christian music that will surely enhance your walk with the Lord.

We also need to become more guarded about what kind of movies and TV programs we watch. Watching movies and television is a popular thing, mainly because it's easy and gratifying to the flesh. Anything that makes your flesh happy, you won't get a fight about doing, like sleeping in, putting off responsibilities, or overeating. It doesn't take long, however, before regret steps in.

Of course, it's okay to relax and watch a movie or television show once in a while—when you can find one worth watching—but let it get out of control (like it becoming an addiction and your standards being lowered) and you will eventually see its effects. Plus, think of all the wasted time. Ephesians 5:16 says to make the most of our opportunities to do good (NLT), to make each minute count (CEV), "because the days are evil."

I've heard some Christians and preachers talk about the strict church rules of the past, like no going to movies and only dressing a certain way. They speak of it in such a negative sense that it seems to have caused so many Christians to use that as an excuse to compromise and conform more and more to the lifestyle of the world. Unfortunately the difference can be seen in their character and morality, as their standards have dropped immensely. It's basically a mistake to throw it *all* out. I think we should just work on more balance, and examine our motives instead.

Don't let the cravings of the flesh control you. You control them! If you've always had a problem being disciplined, you can change that. You can create good habits to replace the bad habits. It just takes repetition for a time, and then you'll begin doing it automatically. You've just got to determine how badly you really want it.

You can discipline your flesh by starving it a little, by cutting back on things in the natural that you know you're having too much of, or that you might be giving too much of your time or attention. It's important to stay disciplined and balanced. Philippians 4:5 says, "Let your moderation be known unto all men. The Lord is at hand" (KJV). That's talking about controlling our flesh and not allowing "excess of craving, or dress, or eating," but governing our appetites.[4]

## Weaken Your Flesh, Strengthen Your Spirit

The flesh has a will of its own. Occasional fasting is a great way to keep your flesh under control. Denying your flesh of little things now and then prepares you to be able to deny it of the bigger temptations that come your way. You could just fast one meal, one day, or a few days, or it could be other things your flesh really likes, such as coffee, dessert, electronics, shopping, or anything else you enjoy.

Don't be confused, thinking you've got to fast (go without food) for 40 days as Jesus did. The fact that Jesus had never sinned (given in to the flesh) and that He was led by the Spirit into the wilderness just after He was baptized and anointed, we can assume that He was mighty strong in Spirit. The Bible says, "*Afterwards* He did hunger" (Matthew 4:2 YLT). That's not the case with the rest of mankind. Our hunger sets in after skipping one meal. Or just the thought of going on a fast can make us hungry. The flesh responds immediately when we're about to do something to strengthen our spirit.

Although Moses and Elijah had fasted 40 days and 40 nights, they were both under supernatural experiences. Moses went without food and water. He was in the very presence of the almighty God. (Deuteronomy 9:9,18.) He had to be very much in the Spirit to be before God like that, especially under the old covenant, where the veil was not yet torn—meaning the access we have into the throne room of God, through Christ, was not yet available. (Matthew 27:51.) It was the presence of God that sustained him.[5] And Elijah had eaten food that the angel of the Lord brought to him. The angel told him that food would give him strength for the journey. The strength of that food lasted 40 days and 40 nights. (1 Kings 19:5–8.) It was definitely a supernatural meal! So, before choosing a complete fast with no food and water, be sure the Holy Spirit is leading you to do that, so that you know He will sustain you as He did in these examples.

Most importantly, when you skip something, replace it with spending time in prayer and reading the Bible. Scriptures about fasting usually include praying. So, instead of gratifying the flesh, you're feeding your spirit.

Whatever you decide you need to do to get ahold of your flesh, be prepared, because your flesh will automatically have fits.

**1 Peter 4:1,2**

**1 Therefore, since Christ suffered for us in the flesh, arm yourselves also with the same mind, for he who has *suffered in the flesh* has ceased from sin,**

**2 that he no longer should live the rest of his time in the flesh for the lusts of men, but for the will of God.**

The point is the flesh suffers because it's not getting its way, but the reward far exceeds the suffering. Resist the temptation to pamper your flesh and give in to it like the world does. The more steady and consistent you are with keeping it under control, the more it will calm down and the easier it will get.

You've got to stay with controlling your flesh to rise above it and win over it. Like with the gym experience, "no pain, no gain." If you lift the lightest weight possible, and only enough reps that are comfortable to do, then you're not going to get very strong. But if you challenge yourself to lift the weight that's not so easy, and to do reps until you feel pain enough that you can't possibly do another, then you will notice how much more you can do later because of the strength you built—and we all know it takes more than one visit to the gym to get there. It takes consistency. The more you go, the stronger you get. Although, it's hard to stay motivated at first, you'll find that the benefits are too great to quit.

It's that way with getting stronger in the Spirit. You can't just spend a little time with God once in a while and expect to win in the battle set against you. As I mentioned earlier, the enemy is at the door ready to meet you after your time with God to challenge you and steal from you what you just received. A one time, great time with God isn't going to be enough. You've got to build your spiritual strength by going in daily and staying until your flesh gives up on trying to pull you out.

### Matthew 6:16–18

16 Moreover, when you fast, do not be like the hypocrites, with a sad countenance. For they disfigure their faces that they may appear to men to be fasting. Assuredly, I say to you, they have their reward.

17 But you, when you fast, anoint your head and wash your face,

18 so that you do not appear to men to be fasting, but to your Father who is in the secret place; and your Father who sees in secret will reward you openly.

In other words, keep your face fresh-looking and your countenance bright, doing your best to hide the fact that you're

fasting. Plus, the rewards from men are just a short time of attention and favor that will fade quickly. In the long run, you'll see
that it's just vanity that becomes nothing but waste. (Proverbs
20:6.) When you "do it heartily, as to the Lord, and not unto
men" (Colossians 3:23 KJV), the reward from God does more
than get His attention and favor; it brings indescribable blessings that endure, and all those around you will witness it.

*Focus on Serving Others*

Another thing that will help keep your spirit strong and
your flesh under is to purpose to do things for others daily. The
freedom we've been given in Christ was not intended for the
flesh, it was intended to serve others. (Galatians 5:13.) Encourage, help, pray, give. Go out of your way. Walk that extra mile.
Especially for those who can't pay you back or that you can't
receive a lot of attention (pat on the back) for serving. Do all
you can anonymously. The reward will be so much greater.

**Matthew 6:1–4**

1 Take heed that you do not do your charitable deeds before
men, to be seen by them. Otherwise you have no reward
from your Father in heaven.

2 Therefore, when you do a charitable deed, do not sound a
trumpet before you as the hypocrites do in the synagogues
and in the streets, that they may have glory from men.
Assuredly, I say to you, they have their reward.

3 But when you do a charitable deed, do not let your left hand
know what your right hand is doing,

4 that your charitable deed may be in secret; and your Father
who sees in secret will Himself reward you openly.

Flesh is selfish and prideful. It wants all the attention, and it wants everything done for it. My oldest son shared with me this quote (said to be by well-known author C. S. Lewis) that I thought was very accurate: "Pride is like bad breath, everyone around knows you have it but you."

When you focus on serving each other in love, and especially on loving God with all your heart and all your decisions, it keeps you from justifying certain things only to please your flesh.

## Be Led by the Spirit

This message is not meant to overwhelm you on things you can't or shouldn't do. Although there are dos and don'ts in the Bible, today's society (and parts of the church world too) wants to stay away from that. They even teach that you shouldn't tell children straight up, don't. They say it's the wrong approach and that it will make our kids worse. Of course it does—it's the automatic response of the flesh. Children just need to be taught about their flesh nature and how to deal with it, starting at a young age.

We do certainly want to point out to children the positives of life and what they *can* do even more so, and definitely get them to focus on what they should be doing (as I shared in the beginning). But there are times we need to let children know what they can't have or do. The Bible tells us that "Open rebuke is better than secret love" (Proverbs 27:5 KJV). It's better to confront them than to passively cater to them because we're afraid to stir up anything. Otherwise, they will grow up rebelling against anyone who tells them no or don't.

I encourage you to look inside yourself and find out what you really want to do (not your flesh, but the real you—your spirit). Just make sure you don't let anything, especially the media, take over all your free time. You can be creative and branch out and seek for things that are clean, edifying fun. There really are plenty! We've all been given certain talents and hobbies, for instance, that we desire and can be good at. And don't think you're too old or it's too late to start anything. It wasn't until I entered my forties that I started playing competitive tennis in leagues and tournaments, and also learned to play chords on the piano.

You can never spend too much time developing and preparing to use the gifts God has given you for His kingdom business. We've all been called and gifted to do something. Even witnessing takes some preparation time. First Peter 3:15 says, "Be ready always to give an answer to every man that asketh you a reason of the hope that is in you with meekness and fear" (KJV). Interaction with your family and other people is definitely not wasting time either, as long as you're building up each other and enjoying each other's company.

The bottom line is to be led by the Guide inside you—the Holy Spirit. (John 16:13.) He'll show you what will help you and what will hurt you. Proverbs 3:6 says, "In *all* your ways acknowledge Him, and He shall direct your paths."

## Peace and Fruits

We've got to set boundaries and disciplines on ourselves in order to live pure godly lives. We certainly don't want to get in bondage about it, but we also don't want to be afraid to upset our flesh. There's a difference. You'll know that difference by the way you feel after the choice you make. If what you chose upsets your flesh, you will feel at peace inside once you do (or don't do) what you decided. If it's bondage, you're never at peace. Keeping yourself tuned in to the Holy Spirit, while shutting off your "thinker" (your mind), and knowing and applying the Word of God, will keep you out of bondage.

Some people say that certain things don't affect them, but check out their fruits. (Matthew 7:16,20; Galatians 5:22–23.) People can grow numb to things about which they once had a conviction. We discussed conviction in an earlier chapter, but ignoring the conviction is what numbs a person. I'm certainly not telling you to go around passing judgments on everyone, but you should not let your influence be based on what others allow.

Remember Abraham's nephew Lot, who was surrounded by immorality and evil in the wicked city where he lived? Look how Lot was affected.

**2 Peter 2:6–8 GW**

6 **God condemned the cities of Sodom and Gomorrah and destroyed them by burning them to ashes. He made those cities an example to ungodly people of what is going to happen to them.**

7 **Yet, God rescued Lot, a man who had his approval. Lot was distressed by the lifestyle of people who had no principles and lived in sexual freedom.**

8 **Although he was a man who had God's approval, he lived among the people of Sodom and Gomorrah. Each day was like torture to him as he saw and heard the immoral things that people did.**

You might be thinking, "Well, that happened in the Old Testament," but notice that this is mentioned in the New Testament, even after the Holy Ghost was poured out. (Acts 2.) Peter was cautioning us to see this as an example.

First Corinthians 15:33 says, "Do not be deceived: 'Evil company corrupts good habits.'" Our choice of influence will affect the ways we talk, act, and live.

There are people who have certain things they may struggle with that others don't, while the others struggle with things that are not a problem for those people. A lot of times it's based on what they allowed in their flesh before, or that came from their family history, such as alcoholism. Everyone has their own issues that they need to guard against—certain things that have more of an effect on them that they need to stay away from, and anything that relates to it. Regardless of each individual circumstance, we all need to remember the "serving others" part, which includes making choices that will not discourage them in their weaknesses. (1 Corinthians 8:9.) We want to make sure our choices are building up and encouraging all those around us.

Follow your own convictions, no matter what everyone else is doing. You may feel alone sometimes, but it will definitely pay off, and you will find that you're really not alone. Be careful, though, about comparing yourself with others.

In 2 Corinthians 10:12, it says, "They measuring themselves by themselves, and comparing themselves among themselves, are not wise." Your focus should never be on how other Christians are living. And especially don't become critical, thinking of yourself as better. Nor do you want to go to the opposite extreme by thinking something must be wrong with you. What you need to compare yourself to is the Word of God. Keep your eyes on the Lord and your ears open to what He's saying to you—and obey Him.

## Guidance and Obedience

Obeying the Lord plays a very important part in keeping your spirit strong and sensitive. Once you know what the Lord is telling you to do or not to do, obey quickly. Hesitation makes room for doubt. You'll start to reason with yourself and with God, and think that maybe that wasn't God, or that it was just your own idea. After doubt enters, you most likely won't do it, but if you do end up doing things in doubt, the outcome won't be what it was suppose to be.

For example, if you were prompted in church to go up to the front for prayer for something when an altar call is given, or you were prompted to pray for someone else, and you wait long enough for it to go from your heart to your head, doubt can stand in your way. You've got to be in faith to receive. The same thing goes when God prompts you to say something to someone, or do something for someone. Put it off and very likely your opportunity will be gone. And waiting for a full explanation of why isn't wise either. A lot of times that will come after you miss it; then you'll want to kick yourself. God wants you to fully trust Him.

God will warn you of things that you shouldn't say or do as well. That requires a quick restraint. If you don't stop yourself, you'll see that the feelings and consequences that follow won't be worth it.

Obeying quickly can also keep you from trouble that's ahead. The Holy Spirit will lead you into safety, and warn you of paths that would harm you. He may even tell you to take a different route home from work. Don't reason, just go! I've heard testimonies of individuals avoiding bad accidents by following that prompting from the Holy Spirit. A number of people didn't go to work at the World Trade Center in New York on September 11, 2001, because they were flexible enough to change their regular plans and routines as they felt prompted. Heeding that inner prompting saved their lives. You've got to stay open and willing to change your schedule.

That prompting or leading comes in a peaceful way, where fear will not be involved, as we saw earlier in 2 Timothy 1:7. If the Holy Spirit is not a Spirit of fear, then He's certainly not going to lead by fear. First Corinthians 14:33 says, "God is not the author of confusion, but of peace." So, if you're feeling confused about direction, know that it is definitely not the way God leads.

The verses below show us that there's no fear or confusion and our mind is sound (disciplined and self-controlled) when the Holy Spirit is leading:

- Isaiah 55:12 says, "For you shall go out with joy, and be led out with peace."

- Colossians 3:15 says, "Let the peace of God rule in your hearts."

- Philippians 4:7 says, "The peace of God, which surpasses all understanding, will guard your hearts and minds through Christ Jesus."

- John 14:27 says, "Peace I leave with you, My peace I give to you; not as the world gives do I give to you. Let not your heart be troubled, neither let it be afraid."

- 1 John 4:18 says, "There is no fear in love; but perfect love casts out fear."

God *is* that perfect love! (1 John 4:8.) He's all about peace. And as you give Him dominion over your life, there will be no room for fear.

Sometimes our own imaginations or thoughts that the enemy brings can stir up fear. That's not God's leading. On the other hand, He may be directing you to do something that might scare you. Just because you respond in fear doesn't mean it wasn't God. The initial leading will be peaceful. Then we have to trust Him and not be afraid to step out and obey.

When God is directing you, there's a confidence that rises on the inside of you about something, and it's strong, yet gentle and peaceful. You'll know in an instant what He's directing you to do or not to do, but bear in mind that you must respond quickly, before your head gets in the way.

On other occasions, when you're seeking for direction on big decisions ahead, and you're not sure yet what God's will is, it's good to take time with Him about it, in prayer and being still in His presence. Be patient and careful not to jump out ahead of God. Wait for His clear direction and right timing. In the Old Testament, when the children of Israel were in the wilderness, God led them with a cloud by day and a pillar of fire by night. They only moved when the cloud/pillar moved. And when it stopped, the children of Israel stopped. (Exodus 13:21.) But now God leads by His Word and His Spirit.

Also, look for confirmation. The answer will come up more than once, usually several times. Remember, when we acknowledge Him, He *will* direct our paths, as He said He would. When you have a variety of choices (such as which church, school, or job to pursue), you should gather information and explore them, expecting to hear a yes or no. He'll direct us as we're on the go, and as we're taking steps.

### Isaiah 30:21

**21 Your ears shall hear a word behind you, saying, "This is the way, walk in it," whenever you turn to the right hand or whenever you turn to the left.**

It's kind of like the old game of hot and cold. When you're moving away from the object you need to find, you're told you're getting cold. So, you turn and head in other directions, until you hear them say you're getting hot, which means you're in the right area. Acts 16:6–10 shows us that as the apostles were traveling, preaching the gospel, the Spirit would stop them from going in the places they shouldn't go. He would also reveal to them where they needed to go.

Romans 8:14 says, "For as many as are led by the Spirit of God, they are the sons of God" (KJV). So, if you have received Jesus as your Lord, then you're a child of God, and the Spirit of God will faithfully lead you. The more you ignore the Holy Spirit, however, the less you'll be tuned in to hear Him. That's a dangerous state to be in. Instant obedience must become a habit.

Do you see why being spirit-controlled instead of flesh-controlled is so important? It's all about sincerely letting Jesus be Lord over your life. Don't let your life just be full of the sacrifices you choose. It's human nature to usually pick convenient sacrifices. Give the Lord a chance to show you what He wants you to do, and then obey Him. Whatever He asks us to do is for our ultimate best. What He chooses is better than what we choose. He sees the whole picture. We don't. He's more into us succeeding than we are. He's trustworthy.

Sacrifices are good, but obedience is better. (1 Samuel 15:22.)

Beware of this: When you're operating in the flesh, the enemy will tempt you by bringing you a thought that you're missing out on so much. He'll try to make you think things like, "Everyone has seen it, or done it. You're out there in left field, being the oddball. What kind of life is this?" The good news is when your spirit is strong you won't care. You will desire the right things. You will know that you're not missing out. Most of all, you'll be happy, content, and completely fulfilled.

There's nothing like living with a clear, clean, and uncluttered conscience. And the things you choose to do will be more enjoyable.

# CHAPTER 12

# Why Are We Still Here?

You might be wondering why this flesh versus spirit warfare is still going on since Jesus has already defeated the devil for us. Why, then, if the enemy has been conquered, are we still here?

While Jesus was on the earth, the things He chose to do the most for the kingdom can be seen in the Gospels (Matthew, Mark, Luke, and John). His life was all about reaching and helping people. *Our reason for still being here on earth is to continue the work that Jesus was doing while He was here, to follow the example He showed us.*

We've been given the total victory over Satan, but the fact is he is still the god of this world until the end of time. So he continues to hang around trying to deceive us and make us doubt that victory, as he did to Eve in the garden. He goes after those with potential to do great things for the kingdom of God to stop them. All who have accepted Jesus as their Lord and Savior have that potential in them.

The important thing is not just to rest in that assurance of why the enemy attacks us so much, but don't let him stop you. Choose to go forth and accomplish mighty things for the kingdom of God.

The greatest thing you can do is to lead people to the Lord. We all have been given the ability and the commission to do that. It's the reason Satan's fate has been delayed. (Genesis 3:15; Revelation 20:10.)

**2 Peter 3:9,15**

   **9 The Lord is not slack concerning His promise, as some count slackness, but is longsuffering toward us, not willing that any should perish but that all should come to repentance . . .**

**15 consider that the longsuffering of our Lord is salvation.**

The *longsuffering* here, I believe, is the evil that God is putting up with, particularly toward His church, and the patience He has for the sake of others having the chance to get saved.

God has compassion on the lost and His desire is for them to come to know Him and His great salvation. When the end comes, it will be too late. So He tells us through the apostle Peter, "Be sober, be vigilant; because your adversary the devil walks about like a roaring lion, seeking whom he may devour" (1 Peter 5:8).

Note the part, "whom he *may* devour." That means the devil has to have your permission. You give him permission to devour you by being consumed "with the cares of this world," and being "unwatchful"[6] of his tactics, as it causes you to believe him and receive his lies, rather than believe what God says.

Verse 9 goes on to say, "Whom resist steadfast in the faith, knowing that the same afflictions are accomplished in your brethren that are in the world" (KJV). The *Message Bible* describes to *resist* here like this: "Keep a cool head. Stay alert . . . Keep your guard up . . . keep a firm grip on the faith."

Resisting Satan involves recognizing him and what he's up to. Not glorify him, just be aware of him. If you don't, he'll deceive you into thinking that it's you or someone else, which will cause guilt, confusion, or division. Avoid that by not being ignorant of his sly ways "lest Satan should get an advantage of [you]" (2 Corinthians 2:11 KJV.) Resist and refuse any space for him, as you hold tight and steady to what you have committed to believe. Remember, faith goes beyond what you're feeling.

The enemy has no power anymore over us who are saved. *The only fight that we have is hanging on to that truth and walking in the victory that belongs to us.* Satan will try to cause you to doubt in your mind and try to convince you that you are defeated. But if you'll just stay a step ahead of him and do things God's way, he will not succeed.

## Reigning Over Your Thoughts

You can't overcome the battle in your mind with your own natural ability. It can only be done *through God*.

**2 Corinthians 10:3–5** KJV

3 **Though we walk in the flesh, we do not war after the flesh:**

4 **(For the weapons of our warfare are not carnal, but mighty *through* God to the pulling down of strong holds;)**

5 **Casting down imaginations, and every high thing that exalteth itself against the knowledge of God, and bringing into captivity every thought to the obedience of Christ.**

The enemy begins his attack by offering thoughts, and your flesh is more than willing to receive them. If the thoughts you are thinking are making you feel discouraged, unhappy, guilty, angry, resentful, hopeless, or other negative emotions, you know they are not lining up with the Word of God. He has redeemed us from all of that. So we have to resist those kinds of thoughts with the Word, and choose to walk in the Spirit.

Whenever wrong thoughts or imaginations come, regardless of your feelings and how real or right on those thoughts seem, if they don't line up with the Word, discard them. Capture them and cast them out immediately. Picture your mind like a computer, iPhone, or iPad, and when a wrong thought or wrong picture appears, just click on the "delete button"—refuse and reject it—and see it quickly disappear into the little "trash can"—into nonexistence. Then go back to your "screen saver"—the mind of Christ.

As wrong thinking comes from our flesh (or the devil), we must deal with it by doing the opposite, as we have already discussed. Think on things that will uplift you and encourage you and keep your spirit strong. Make your thoughts obey the Lord and line up with His Word.

**1 Peter 1:13** GW

**13 Therefore, your minds must be clear and ready for action. Place your confidence completely in what God's kindness [grace and favor] will bring you when Jesus Christ appears again.**

We are responsible for renewing our minds. It has to be done throughout each day because that's where the battle starts. We talked about this, but it bears repeating. It's up to us to keep control of what thoughts we allow or embrace, but we not only have the Word of God to change us on the inside (which produces outward change);[7] we have the Holy Spirit's help with it[8] and with everything else we do that's of God. (Zechariah 4:6; 1 Peter 1:2 GW.) We *can* keep a reign on our thoughts.

Wrong thoughts will try to come, but we can fight them off through God's Word and His ability. The way we accomplish that is by keeping our mind full of the Word, speaking out scriptures, and going to the throne room for strength.

## Jump-Start the Day

Shortly after the resurrection of Jesus, He was taken up to Heaven. He is now seated at the right hand of God, forever praying for us and working with us and in us. (Hebrews 7:25.)

### Hebrews 4:14,15 KJV

14 Seeing then that we have a great High Priest, that is passed into the heavens, Jesus the Son of God, let us hold fast our profession.

15 For we have not an High Priest which cannot be touched with the feeling of our infirmities; but was in all points tempted like as we are, yet without sin.

The Lord is not just sitting up there on the judgment seat watching us to see whether we're going to get it right or not. He is always interceding for us. He's more on our side, fighting for us, than we realize. (Psalm 118:6.) Grasping this truth will definitely boost your confidence and give you boldness to come into God's presence.

### Hebrews 4:16 KJV

16 Let us therefore come boldly unto *the throne of grace* that we may obtain mercy, and find grace to help in time of need.

The *Amplified Bible, Classic Edition,* version of this verse describes God's throne of grace as "the throne of God's unmerited favor to us." It's so important to daily go into the throne room and spend time with God to get what we need (spiritually and otherwise) to conquer victoriously. This is one major responsibility of ours, as Christians. When you do that faithfully, it will help you fulfill all other responsibilities, such as walking in integrity, being a godly and productive parent, spouse, boss, employee, or student.

My goal has always been to spend time with the Lord in the morning, before anyone gets up in my house, because once they start getting up, the demands of the day begin. I need to prepare ahead of time for those demands by fueling up on God's grace. Plus, my mind is so much clearer in the morning; it does not have as many distracting thoughts. Do keep in mind it's not so much about spending time with God before you do anything else. It's about making time with God the most important part of your day. That's what causes Him to become your number one priority.

Our time that we set aside to spend alone with God, and going into His throne room is like the jump-start for the day. It's imperative that we be sure we don't leave Him there, only for that section of our day. We've got to take Him with us throughout the whole day. What I mean by that is to stay sensitive to His presence, continually communing with Him and acknowledging Him, making Him Lord over our every thought, word, action, and decision. If we're not careful, our little morning devotional can become a ritual or a religious, self-righteous act where, after we spend some time with the Lord, we walk away feeling good about ourselves in a prideful way. Then we wonder why we're so weak.

Our need for God and keeping ourselves mindful of Him is just as important as the air we breathe. Thinking of it that way, we can also consider that there's nothing to be proud about when we're just breathing air. Our oxygen certainly didn't come from anything we did. It's free. And so is our fellowship with God. Well, it does cost a little time, but somehow, when we sow that time, He causes our time to be extended. It's amazing how it works.

I know by experience (and have talked to others who have experienced the same) that when we make time for God, we always have enough time to get the things done that we need to do for that day. On the other hand, when we don't make time for God, we usually end up running out of time to do what we need to do. It's about the law of sowing and reaping. (Galatians 6:7.) You sow time, you reap time.

## Be an Open Vessel

This is something else we see in the four Gospels—Jesus often took time to get alone and pray. Sometimes He would pray all night, and sometimes very early in the morning, before the sun came up. Even He needed that time alone with God to handle the demands of His day.

Jesus was often surrounded by a crowd that was so hungry and desperate to be freed from various kinds of bondage—sickness, disease, oppression, poverty, and others. Some were just seeking the security of a good shepherd.

### Mark 6:31–34

31 [Jesus] said unto them, "Come aside by yourselves to a deserted place and rest a while." For there were many coming and going, and they did not even have time to eat.

32 So they departed to a deserted place in the boat by themselves.

33 But the multitudes saw them departing, and many knew Him and ran there on foot from all the cities. They arrived before them and came together to him.

34 And Jesus, when He came out, saw a great multitude and was moved with compassion for them, because they were like sheep not having a shepherd. So He began to teach them many things.

Jesus was trying to get a little break for Himself and His disciples, but notice His amazing and selfless attitude. Instead of complaining about their short time out in the ship, He was moved by what the multitude went through to get to Him. Jesus cared about every detail and need. His disciples told Him to send the multitude away because it was late and they needed to go buy themselves some food, but Jesus was aware that it would be too long of a journey for some of them. That's when He performed one of the miracles of feeding thousands with very little food. (Mark 8:1–9.)

Jesus never turned anybody away that sought after Him. His compassion was so great. He was never focused on His own personal needs. His heart was so set on meeting others' needs—and He still takes pleasure in meeting them. Now He does all these things through people. To be that open vessel for Him to use should be one of our utmost goals.

We are not here to just keep our heads above water while we wait for the return of Jesus. We do have responsibilities as we wait. The amazing thing is that as you fulfill these responsibilities you will find yourself way above water, more like walking on water.

Jesus had appeared to several people after He was raised from the dead. He gave instructions to the believers, mainly to preach the gospel (which is His story and what He did) to the whole world, and to do what He did—heal the sick, raise the dead, cast out devils. If you are a believer, Jesus said these signs will follow you, including the sign of speaking with new tongues. (Mark 16:17–18.)

Jesus also said, "Freely you have received, freely give" (Matthew 10:8). He wants everyone to receive this free gift of eternal life.

### John 3:16, 17

16 For God so loved the world that He gave His only begotten Son, that *whoever* believes in Him should not perish but have everlasting life.

17 For God did not send his Son into the world to condemn the world, but that the world through Him might be saved.

It's not our job to condemn either. It's our job to reach out and rescue them, giving them what we have been given—endless mercy and compassion.

Always make yourself available for Jesus, willing to have your own schedule interrupted. Walk as He walked, love as He loves, and see people the way He does. He will surely help you do that if you ask Him. I have asked Him many times to help me see people through His eyes of compassion, and He has. I can't even describe just how great that feels, to have your mind totally off of yourself and your own needs and on to others and their needs. And then to see just how much more your own needs get met.

Here's the point. Defeating Satan is not our responsibility. Jesus already defeated him. Rescuing souls from the enemy's traps—taking the keys of the kingdom that we have and unlocking their prison doors by revealing to them the same truth that rescued us—is our responsibility as long as we are on this earth. (Matthew 16:19.)

Our big fight is to not let the devil, or our flesh, stop us. The more our spirit is built up, the greater affect we will have on the world.

# CHAPTER 13

# Staying on Top

Every day there are certain things we have to do to take care of ourselves: eat, sleep, shower, brush our teeth, do laundry, clean, cook, work, to name a few. We might get tired of doing some of those things, but since we know they have to get done we do them anyway. To have a greater affect on this world for God and remain stable in our walk with Him, we need to have this same attitude about dealing with our flesh. It should be done on a daily basis in order to stay on top and walk uprightly.

Earlier we talked about putting on the whole armor of God, and using the right weapons to stay strong in the Lord and not live according to our feelings. The Bible clearly shows us other things we need to put on to live that way.

Romans 13:14 tells us, "Put on the Lord Jesus Christ, and make no provision for the flesh, to fulfill its lusts." In other words, put on the character of Christ and don't provide the flesh with what it needs to have what it's lusting after— "don't let yourself think about ways to indulge your evil desires" (v. 14 NLT).

Reasoning with our flesh is not an option. We can't give it any chances or opportunities because we will never overcome temptation *in* our flesh. It's like the old saying, "If you play with fire, you *will* get burned!" We overcome temptation through walking in the Spirit, following our heart, and following the Word of God. Here are some more things the Bible tells us to put on—and some to put off—to control our flesh:

Ephesians 4:22–24

22 *Put off,* concerning your former conduct [lifestyle], the old man which grows corrupt according to the deceitful lusts,

23 and be renewed in the spirit of your mind,

24 and that you *put on* the new man which was created according to God, in true righteousness and holiness.

Colossians 3:8–10,12

8 Now you yourselves are to *put off* all these; anger, wrath, malice, blasphemy, filthy language out of your mouth.

9 Do not lie to another, since you have *put off* the old man with his deeds,

10 and have *put on* the new man, who is renewed in knowledge according to the image of Him who created him . . .

12 Therefore, as the elect of God, holy and beloved, *put on* tender mercies, kindness, humility, meekness, longsuffering.

One translation of the original Greek word for "put on" is "clothe one's self."[9] It's like changing clothes—simply taking off and putting on. Take off the rags (bad behavior) and put on the new clothes (good behavior). It all boils down to what we've been talking about—walking in the Spirit, not in the flesh. (Romans 8:1,4.)

Notice what we are addressed as in the Colossians 3 verse. Think of it: before we take off and put on we already are chosen "of God, holy and beloved." It's not that we're trying to be these things; we already are. It's like the clothes you wear on your physical body do not change who you are. But just as it is more fitting for a prince or princess to dress in fine, costly attire (it's part of what reveals their position), so it is for the Christian to put on this good behavior. The instructions we're given in the New Testament are to show us how we ought to live since we are made righteous. It is possible for us to operate in this lifestyle with the help of the Holy Spirit in us. This is what *The People's New Testament* Bible commentary says about putting on from Romans 13:14: "To put on Christ is to enter into fellowship with Him. He who is in fellowship with Christ cannot fulfill the lusts of the flesh. 'He walks after the Spirit, and not after the flesh'."[10] We've got to keep the communication lines between the Lord and us open 24/7.

I used to get so discouraged when I would see all the areas in which I was not measuring up. Now that I understand the truth more clearly, I'm grateful for being able to see the things I need to work on and improve. It's better for me to see it than everyone else but me. And for God to show it to me reveals that He is at work in me. It's with the Word that He corrects us.

**2 Timothy 3:16,17 KJV**

**16 All scripture is given by inspiration of God, and is profitable for doctrine, for reproof, for correction, for instruction in righteousness:**

**17 that the man of God may be perfect, thoroughly furnished unto all good works.**

The word perfect here refers to being complete and equipped. The Bible also tells us that God corrects those He loves. (Proverbs 3:12.) That's quite encouraging. God's Word not only trains and equips us, it corrects us so that we "are completely prepared to do good things" (2 Timothy 3:17 GW). So if you stand corrected over an area that you messed up in and didn't keep on top quite the way you should have, just repent (remember, that's turning around and going in a different direction), pick up where you are, do what you know to do, and start afresh.

When a baby learns to walk he falls a lot, but he doesn't stay down and decide to crawl the rest of his life. He naturally gets right back up without even thinking about it. It's so important to see that we need to handle our circumstances this way. We've got to quickly make the correction. We are in charge, concerning our flesh. We no longer have to be held down or controlled by it.

## You Are Approved!

It's also important that we don't waste time wallowing in guilt over messing up or over feelings of defeat. That's just what the devil wants you to do. Feelings of being disapproved of by God will hinder you from making the necessary corrections. It will keep you in a rut. Your actions might have been disapproved of, but you are not!

We are approved by the blood of Jesus, not our works. We have to truly believe that if we confess our sins, Jesus will forgive us of our sins and cleanse us from all unrighteousness, just as He said He would. (1 John 1:9.) Do we really believe it or not?

If our own children do wrong and they come to us later and say they're sorry, it warms our hearts and we forgive them. We can be assured that God responds like that. There are many scriptures where He compares His love for us to a natural father towards his son. We are literally His children, and He wants us to relate to Him as our Father. Approach Him the same way you would approach a perfect dad, because that's what He is.

One night, while in church, during praise and worship, I asked God how my heart looked to Him, and I instantly saw in my mind's eye Jesus coming and standing in front of me. God was showing me that He sees the heart of Jesus. It can't get any better than that! And you can't get more approved of than that. It's all from the work of the cross, certainly not our own works.

David trusted in God in every circumstance, no matter how great his enemy was. His heart was very tender towards God. You can see that in his writings in Psalms. Yet there was a time when his weakness was challenged, and David sinned against God. He was caught off guard and his flesh began to lust for something he spotted. Without thinking about it, as he was totally in the flesh, he fell. But when he snapped out of it and realized how great a sin he had committed, as it was pointed out to him by a prophet, he humbled himself and sincerely repented. Still, there were consequences for the choices he made. (See 2 Samuel 11, 12.)

We try to do what the Word says yet when we don't, God still never leaves us or stops loving us, but there are consequences we'll have to face. Galatians 6:8 says, "He who sows to his flesh will of the flesh reap corruption, but he who sows to the Spirit will of the Spirit reap everlasting life." When you give in to the flesh, you suffer loss; but if you follow the Spirit, you receive gain.

David earnestly hoped that the consequences would be taken away. Although they weren't, he endured them, then pulled himself together, putting the past behind, and moved forward, serving the Lord and making better choices. God blessed him tremendously after that.

Second Samuel 11:27 says, "The thing that David had done displeased the Lord." Even though the deed displeased God, He still loved David, and the Bible tells us that David was a man after God's own heart. (Acts 13:22.) So, as David did, when you recognize your sin, repent quickly. Don't waste time in regret. You have to learn to live in the moment, even if your mistake or your letdown was five minutes ago. What are you going to do at this moment? Have you repented (turned away from it), or cast your care on the Lord? Now what choice are you going to make? That's what matters.

Hanging on to guilt or regret doesn't prove repentance. It just keeps you weighted down so you can't do anything. We honestly don't have time for that. There's so much that God wants to do in us and through us. Don't insult Him by acting like the sacrifice and blood of His Son, Jesus, isn't enough. Or that Jesus didn't really have to come to take on our sins, as if we should have been able to walk perfectly on our own. Just receive what He did, repent, and move on. To *repent*, as we've seen, is to change your mind, change your direction. Just keep your heart right and set on growing.

## There's Still Mercy

Psalm 147:11 says, "The LORD takes pleasure in those who fear Him, in those who hope in His mercy." Now, *fear* here refers to reverence. When we think about pleasing the Lord, we usually think of having the right attitude, doing the right things, and of course, reverencing Him. But verse 11 tells us of something else that pleases Him, and that is, hoping in His mercy. You may be hard on yourself and feel like you've made the same mistake or have blown it too many times and you wonder if there is any more mercy left for you. If so, you most likely feel this way because you really want to please God. Let these scriptures encourage you.

**Proverbs 24:16** AMP

**16 A righteous man falls seven times, and rises again.**

The key is to get right back up.

**Lamentations 3:22,23** KJV

**22 It is of the Lord's mercies that we are not consumed, because his compassions fail not.**

**23 They are new every morning: great is thy faithfulness.**

As long as you're alive, there's still mercy for you—if you want it. So, take this moment you have and do something worthwhile. Worship God. It's not something for you to deserve. It's for Him, and He always deserves it!

Remember that living with guilt does not please God, but hoping in His mercy does. Then keep hoping and believing in His Word for change.

# CHAPTER 14

# The Way to Succeed

By now you may have thought, "I've read so many books, heard so many sermons, and prayed so many prayers. Why am I not totally changed?" You might even go off by yourself for a few days to get alone with God and fast and pray. I'm sure that would be a great experience, and you could even have some breakthroughs, but it won't stop issues of the flesh from showing up.

Change is a daily process that will continue until Jesus comes back. All these things (the books, sermons, prayers, and fasting) are good to do and will help, but it's about consistency in keeping ourselves built up in the Word and choosing to continually act on what we've learned, making them our *lifestyle*.

The more you do what the Word says and say no to your flesh on a regular basis, the easier it gets. In the last chapter, we talked about physical things we have to do daily to keep up our bodies, homes, cars, and other possessions. Although we wash ourselves, our cars, or clean our houses, they're not going to stay clean on their own. Dust and dirt continue to show up, but we won't hardly see it if we keep them clean regularly. It's the same principle with working out and eating.

When you work out for a while, once you see the results you want, you can't just quit and expect your body to stay that way. You've got to be consistent and continue working out to maintain it. Likewise, when your body needs food, you feed it. About a few hours after eating you're hungry again, and you're usually quick to take care of that problem. Many of us are very consistent about that! If only we can be that way when our spirit is hungry again, by being quick to give it the kind of "food" it needs.

A steady spiritual diet will keep us on the right path with the right attitude.

When you're spending time in prayer with the Lord and you're really enjoying His presence, it's so easy to make the decision to change in areas that need it. And you're truly sincere about it. In no time at all, however, as you go along your way, you'll be challenged. You'll have the opportunity to prove whether you really meant what you said when you were "feeling" so good. Feelings come and go, and when they're not there, faith by your works has to step in. Your actions, especially when you don't feel like it, reveal the extent of your commitment.

First Thessalonians 2:4 tells us that God tries our hearts. He doesn't bring temptation along, but as we face the things that are challenging our decision, He sees how committed we really are about making the change. And He's so faithful to supply the strength we need, as we depend on Him for it. Every time you meet that challenge I encourage you to look at it as a chance to perfect the change.

Remember, even if you didn't quite pass the test, don't get discouraged; just be ready for the next opportunity, knowing you can do it and you will do it, with God's help. You're able to and you choose to!

Applying this principle can bring success to any area of life. I have even found this to be true in my tennis matches. I've learned that my attitude often determines how well I play, and that the challenge is more on the mental side than the physical side. When I would get upset at myself for making a mistake in a match, I would just continue to make them until I finally learned that it was the frustration that would make me choke, and then lose. I learned the importance of focusing on playing in the moment, the present point, and forgetting about the score and the last point. Now when I make a mistake, I just ask myself what I did wrong and decide what adjustment I need to make. Then I expect to win the next point.

I've also learned the importance of allowing no emotion, such as anger, anxiety, self-pity or pride. It's not that we won't feel emotions; it's that we don't grab hold of them and run with them. Actually the opponent on the other side of the net isn't necessarily the competition as much as I am. My main challenge is not to let anything hold me back from playing the best that I can.

A great example of that is when my daughter was playing in a tennis tournament at age 11. She lost by far, but she played really well. After the match, I was prepared to encourage her, thinking she was going to need it. She came off the court with a big smile on her face, saying, "That was the best match I've ever played! I feel really good about how well I did." That is a winning attitude. She was the consolation winner in the next tournament she played in after that.

To remain steady and confident is the main key to win. My game was totally turned around once I began applying these principles. What has been even more exciting is realizing that I can apply them to other more important areas of my life and not choke at opposition, but instead, meet it head-on and win!

The devil is our opponent. He's the one who wants to convince us that we are losers, and that we are rejected. With a competitive attitude we've got to be determined to prove that he is wrong. We are *winners*, and we are *accepted*!

## Believe the Right Thing

Over seventeen years ago I had entered a major competition with the enemy. It was his symptoms against my faith. After my third healthy child, I had two miscarriages within a year. They totally caught me off guard. I was not prepared for that attack and I gave in to the symptoms. I didn't put up much of a fight because it had already looked hopeless.

I couldn't stand the thought of ending in defeat. A couple years later I got pregnant again. After taking the home test very early in the morning and seeing that the result was positive, I went into a room by myself and dropped to my knees and said, "Lord, I've got to win this time. I've got to have the final victory in this area." His presence was very close and real, and I had the assurance that I would win, but I knew my faith would be challenged.

Then the thought came to me, "Oh no, I went horseback riding the other day, and the horse ran and trotted." I immediately felt impressed to not even talk about that. The devil was trying to slip fear in right away.

It wasn't long at all before the symptoms of miscarriage began to hit. I hadn't gone to my first doctor appointment yet, so I called there later that afternoon to let them know what I was experiencing, and the nurse suggested that I go to the ER. Well, our church was having a praise and worship service that night and I really wanted to attend. There was no time to go to the ER before the service, so I decided to go to church. Now, I'm not suggesting that you go against your doctor's orders, but in that instance I felt led to go to the service first.

As I was walking in I had to keep stopping because of the cramping, but once I got in there and started worshiping, the cramping let up some. The presence of the Lord was so strong in that place. Being in the middle of that was exactly what I needed for a good boost for what was ahead. It helped confirm the assurance of winning that I had received from the Lord in the very beginning.

When I went to my doctor appointment soon after, he told me (after seeing the results of the sonogram) that my body was trying to miscarry, so he put me on bed rest. I stood on many scriptures, doing my very best not to talk about the way I felt. When feeling strong cramping I wanted to say, "I'm about to lose this baby," (which is what I would have not hesitated to say before), but by the grace of God I was able to speak positive things, such as, "No weapon that is formed against me shall prosper." (Isaiah 54:17.)

The enemy had thrown so many negative thoughts my way, even the thought that there's probably something wrong with the baby, and that's why my body's trying to miscarry. But the Holy Spirit lead me to just the right scripture—Psalm 138:8— that says, "The Lord will perfect that which concerns me; Your mercy, O Lord, endures forever; do not forsake the works of

Your hands." Still, a couple of times I broke and began to cry, saying to my husband, "I know that I will win, but I'm just tired of the fight."

Talk about a lesson in consistency. That was a big one—but it paid off because we did win! I bore a beautiful little girl who is now 17 years old and has a genuine heart to serve the Lord. She's had a desire to teach since she was a toddler: she got filled with the Holy Spirit at the age of three, and has been eager to share the gospel since she was five. No wonder the enemy put up such a fight, but "Thanks be unto God, which always causeth us to triumph in Christ" (2 Corinthians 2:14 KJV)!

It's not just about always saying the right thing; it's definitely got to be mixed with always believing the right thing. We don't speak out the scriptures as a magic formula or an act of our own works, trying to earn it. We speak them out to declare and strengthen our confidence of the truth. It builds up the faith we need to take hold of what belongs to us according to the Word.

## Don't Give Up

Consistency is also required to break certain habits. If you're used to drinking soda every day, then every day your flesh will automatically crave soda. If you decide you want to quit, the desire for it won't go away until you have consistently said no to it for several days or even weeks. But you will one day realize that you no longer want any. In fact, it won't even taste as good to you anymore. You can't be wishy-washy about it either or you won't get to that place. That's how you change. You can create your own habits, good or bad.

When some people who have been addicted to drugs, alcohol, pornography, and/or other things first get saved, they are instantly delivered from those addictions. Others in that situation have to overcome addictions as they learn and grow in the Lord. Every individual is different, but God acknowledges determination, and He will help you where you're at with what you need.

In my last two years of high school, I was running from God and developed an addiction to cigarette smoking as well as other things. When I turned my life back to God, I was instantly delivered from some of them, but others took effort to rid out of my life. It was easy to quit smoking at that time because I was pregnant (as I mentioned earlier) and the smell of cigarette smoke made me nauseous.

Months after my son was born, I was occasionally around smokers. At first, I thought, "I'll never go back there," but the craving was overwhelming. Then one day I thought, "Just one puff." That's all it took, and I was back in the battle of trying to quit again.

That one puff, one taste, one try, one look, is never worth it.

While at the store, I would buy some cigarettes. Then at home, a lot of times while reading my Bible, such conviction would come and I would throw the cigarettes away. This cycle went on for weeks. I wanted so badly to quit, and I sought the Lord much about it. Finally one day I was thinking about and anticipating a revival that I was planning to attend that evening. I had never heard this evangelist before, but I was prompted all day to say to myself and to others that something great was going to happen that night.

Towards the end of the evening service, as the preacher was beginning to give the altar call, he called me to come up (I had just been praying and deciding that I was going to throw the cigarettes away again, and that I would overcome this). The Lord said to me, through the preacher, that He was going to remove the stumbling block and that hindrance that's been in my way. So, after service, I went home and threw the cigarettes out for the last time. As I released them I felt the power of God all over me. I never again craved a cigarette. I was totally delivered!

Key factors are not only our determination and our consistency, but also our expectation. Speak out what you're expecting and picture the end results you want. God always meets us half way. Actually, He goes much farther. So don't give up! You never know how close you are to your breakthrough!

## Walk with the Lord

The stronger we are in the Spirit, the less we'll give in to the flesh. Having a close walk with the Lord is what strengthens us in the Spirit. Remember, we walk with Him when we read the Word, obey it, spend time alone with Him talking, praying, and worshiping Him, praying in our heavenly prayer language, and acknowledging Him throughout the day. Doing those things develops our relationship with Him, and will help us tremendously in dealing with our flesh. There are many awesome benefits that follow this way of living.

The closer I walk with God, not only does more revelation knowledge open up to me about His Word, and I can see and understand more in the Spirit realm; but also more things are revealed in my flesh nature that are disturbing. It's like our spirit becomes a flashlight, exposing the darkness of the flesh.

It seems as though after working on and getting somewhat of a handle on one thing, something else shows up. I realize that if I'll consistently crucify my flesh[11] and keep it (what I see) under control, by seeking the Lord on how to deal with it, and finding out what I should be doing or how I should be thinking or acting; I have less trouble with it, and I'm able to overcome each one so much quicker.

To be totally delivered from having to deal with the trouble our flesh causes will only happen when we leave this earthly body. We don't want to get in a hurry to do that, though, because God needs us here to reach out to the lost and encourage other believers. When the time comes when we stand before the Lord, beholding His amazing beauty, there will be nothing more satisfying then hearing our Lord Jesus say, "Well done, good and faithful servant . . . Enter into the joy of your Lord" (Matthew 25:21). "For what is our hope, or joy, or crown of rejoicing? Is it not even you in the presence of our Lord Jesus Christ at His coming?" (1 Thessalonians 2:19 CEV). I imagine, just as the twenty-four elders, we will be casting our crowns (rewards) before the throne, saying, "You are worthy, O Lord, to receive glory and honor and power" (Revelation 4:10–11).

Keeping these things in mind will surely make our struggles seem insignificant and will help us to spend our time more wisely, doing the things that matter. We have the power to choose what we do and don't do—and what we hold on to and what we let go of. We have the ability to lay aside the things we keep tripping on. The Lord wouldn't tell us to do it if we couldn't. He is just. Believe it, and press on!

CHAPTER 15

# The Absolute Best

The things we go through are so minor compared to the things Jesus went through here on earth. Remember, He was clothed in the same kind of flesh that we are. He felt the same kind of temptations. He had to war off the same kind of thoughts and feelings that we do. He also had the same five senses.

Even the night before the crucifixion, as Jesus was seeing the pain and suffering that was ahead—not just the physical pain, but also the pain of being temporarily separated from His Father God because of our sin that was going to be put on Him—He began to sweat great drops of blood. That is the highest level of stress. Yet as you read the Gospels and follow His examples, you'll see that He was continually watching and praying. He endured it all because of the joy of what was beyond the hardship. (Hebrews 12:2.) Because He endured, He conquered death, hell and the grave for us—and His very nature, strength, and ability now abide in us who believe.

It's so important to keep your eyes on the rewards that follow this flesh versus spirit battle, just as Jesus did, knowing that you are already a guaranteed winner. At the end of the apostle Paul's life here on earth, he said, "I have fought a good fight" (2 Timothy 4:7 KJV). It's a good fight because we win!

Paul also said, "I press toward the mark for the prize of the high calling of God in Christ Jesus" (Philippians 3:14 KJV). The enemy, Satan, will do his best to throw obstacles in your way to get you off your path, off focus, or to get you to stop pressing on. Some obstacles may seem to make you feel alone, uncared for, and abandoned. You may feel totally defeated, thinking, "This one's too big. I can't handle it." It may seem, at times, like God has let you down and you don't see how you can go on. How do you trust? How do you believe again? You did the things you thought you knew to do. What happened?

For one thing, Satan wants you to get in this exact mindset. Sometimes you just have to step outside of yourself and see the battle that's really going on. You have to just set aside the whys for another time. The answers do eventually come, as you seek the Lord. Some may not come until you get to Heaven, but then you won't even care.

After you set the whys aside, you must push through with a strong determination, refusing to fall back and retreat. Refuse to believe the lies of the enemy and your flesh. Go against those overwhelming emotions and mental anguish. Do not go by your own observation and diagnosis.

I had to do these things several years ago when I lost my dad. That was just about my toughest experience ever. So, I write this with heartfelt understanding and an urgency to help and comfort you in whatever you may be going through with the same comfort I received from the Lord and others. (2 Corinthians 1:3–4).

## The Decision to Trust

My dad was diagnosed with brain cancer, and died about two and a half months later. When I first found out he had passed away, I was bombarded by many emotions, and I said, "What now, Lord? How will I be able to lay hands on the sick and pray and expect them to recover? My faith is crushed."

As I was dealing with the frustration, I heard on the inside, *You just need to win someone to Christ.* That thought did not come from me because I was in the middle of overwhelming grief, wondering how I was going to get through this. My response was, "Revenge, huh?" That helped me to stay aware of whom I'm up against. It's certainly not God.

The following week while I was ministering with a group of women in the jail (I do jail ministry through my church), a lady came in after we were done having a service and said to me, "I was told to come in here. Will you pray for me? My daughter is missing and no one knows where she is." First, I asked her if she was a Christian, and she said no. So, I shared the gospel with her, and asked her if she wanted to receive Jesus; she said yes. After she did, we prayed for her daughter (I would have prayed for her daughter anyway, but her own salvation was important too).

The next week when I arrived at the jail, that woman was in the room where we hold the service. She looked at me with a big smile and said, "They found my daughter the next day. I knew they would after we prayed." I believe that her receiving Jesus is what helped her to know that. That was my first step on the road to recovery.

About a week later there was another lady in the jail who was having an issue with her eye, and she asked for prayer. I didn't think about it, I just prayed for her, and she was healed. The Holy Spirit helped me to react without thinking because if I would have thought about it, I would have considered my circumstance with my dad and would have probably questioned too much, which would have opened the door for doubt. God knew how much I needed that experience. The Lord is faithful to help you through any circumstance with opportunities to pray for and minister to others.

All I thought about during those first few weeks after my dad passed was, "I can't stop, I have to push through this; I've got to keep going regardless of how I feel." In most cases it's normal and understandable to take a break from things you're involved in while you're adjusting to the initial shock of loss. But I knew if I stopped I could fall into depression and lose the ground I had gained before the tragedy. During one of my intense grieving moments, all I could do was cry out over and over again, "I don't understand, but I trust You, Lord!" To be totally honest, I wasn't exactly "feeling" that I trusted Him, but it was a decision I was making.

I know that losing my dad to cancer was not God's plan. There are too many scriptures that prove it. It's the thief who comes to steel, kill, and destroy. Jesus has come to give us abundant life, and to heal all our diseases. (John 10:10; Acts 10:38.) My issue was why didn't my dad receive healing? I laid my hands on him and prayed for him, according to Mark 16:18. It seems it can be harder to believe when it's a close friend or family member because of the emotion and fear involved.

This two and a half month battle was so much like a ride on a roller coaster. When I got word of the tumor on his brain, I spent the day going from crying my eyes out to calling out to God in faith. The presence of the Lord was with me, however, and His compassion was strongly felt. A dear, faithful friend of mine also helped me so much during this time, especially that day. I had to call her at least a couple of times. I remember the second time I called, I said to her, "I'm sorry, I'm down again. Can you help me back up?" Her powerful prayer of faith and most gracious words helped me get on my feet, ready to believe again.

The decision was made that evening to go ahead and do brain surgery on my dad. It was extremely risky because of the size and the location of the tumor. So I got alone with God and had a real heartfelt talk with Him. I asked Him to give the surgeon wisdom and to keep His hand on the surgeon's hand. I said, "I've got to see my dad again." I was in Oklahoma and he was in California. So, I went to bed that night at peace, believing that God would do it. I woke up many times through the night, knowing my dad was in the middle of surgery; tempted to be afraid, I would just say, "What's there to fear if God's hand is on the surgeon's hand?" and I would go back to sleep.

Early the next morning I got word that he survived the surgery, but they couldn't guarantee that he would wake up, and if he did, there was a chance he wouldn't know anyone and could be in a vegetable state. Later that morning, when the doctor went in to check on him, to the doctor's surprise, he was wide awake and began talking to him. At one point during that first morning after surgery the nurse saw my dad from a distance, pulling his breathing tube out. She ran in, much panicked, but he was okay, as he continued breathing on his own.

I flew out the next day and went straight to the hospital. I walked in his room and he was sitting up in a chair and he called me by my first and middle name, which he always did. What a relief and a major blessing that was! A week after the brain surgery, he was well enough to go home. He seemed to be getting better, but about the third day, something went wrong and we had to call an ambulance. An infection had developed in his brain and also blood clots in his leg and lung. From that night on into the entire day following he was unconscious, and it really looked like it was over. I remember my grandma and a couple of other friends just before they died, and it was exactly the same.

The heaviness and sorrow were more than I could bear, but as I was out and stuck in traffic trying to get back to the hospital, it dawned on me how I had gotten out of faith and into fear, accepting defeat. I began to pray in the Spirit and worship God, which picked me up out of that and helped me boldly say, "When I get to the hospital, I am going to lay my hand on him in the name of Jesus and he's going to snap out of this." So, I did. When I touched him, he kind of jumped, like it startled him. He had been poked and prodded all day by medical staff and showed no response, but from that moment on he began to come around. When I came back in the morning, he was sitting up, very much alert and eating.

A couple days later I had to fly back home. He was still in the hospital and still doing well, and not long after, he went back home again. Then something else happened, and he was back in the hospital. That happened a few times. My stepmom said every trip seemed to weaken him more and more. Finally, they decided to keep him home and turn to hospice.

He just went downhill from there, so I flew back and sat by his side. He was down to a whisper and hardly opened his eyes, but yet still seemed somewhat peaceful. As I played him a CD of one of my pastor's sermons, I asked him if he wanted or needed anything, and he responded in an aggravated whisper, "I'm trying to hear what the guy's saying! How am I supposed to hear if you keep talking?" I laughed, glad that he was tuned in and listening. Why he ended up dying I don't totally under-stand—but I do know that God is good and He is faithful.

We don't always know what's going on in the person dealing with the sickness. Deaths that are instant and unexpected often can't be explained. There are details we simply don't know. We just need not to take lives for granted, to reach out to those around us with the gospel of salvation, and keep believing that God's Word is true, even when it seems things don't make sense in the natural. And, as I've already mentioned, we need to stay sensitive to the Holy Spirit so that we can be aware of any warnings He may be giving us concerning things ahead. I have heard of various circumstances of Christians who ignored the warnings from the Holy Spirit, and they found themselves in disastrous situations.

## The Better Win

A little over a month before my dad's diagnosis, I was out there for a family reunion and could tell he was not himself. He seemed tired, frustrated, forgetful, and very distant. He also had made several comments that referred to him not being around much longer. He knew something was wrong, and it seemed like he was preparing to go home to be with the Lord. If a person loses their will to go on or their faith to pull through, they will eventually go.

The apostle Paul knew when his ministry was over here. He made it clear, saying,

2 Timothy 4:6,7 KJV

6 I am now ready to be offered, and the time of my departure is at hand.

**7 I have fought a good fight, I have finished my course, I have kept the faith.**

At an earlier time he talked about being torn between staying here and going on to be with Christ. He said that to be with Christ is far better (for him), but to stay was more needful for others. (Philippians 1:21–24.) The Bible shows us how at that time he chose to stay: "Being confident of this, I know that I shall remain and continue with you all for your progress and joy of faith" (v. 25).

I've heard many stories of people hanging on for the sake of their loved ones. What made it obvious that the dying persons wanted to go on to Heaven was that when their loved ones told them they released them to go, the individuals went. Another thing to look at is the fact that in a lot of cases in the Bible where people died, including Jesus, it says they "gave up the ghost" (Mark 15:37 KJV, for instance). I imagine that with all that Jesus had suffered, He could have died long before He did, but He had to carry it all the way through to complete the work. He was "obedient unto death, even the death of the cross" (Philippians 2:8 KJV).

There's a possibility that my dad was tired and ready to go home. He spent years serving the Lord, doing so much for the kingdom of God. He had experienced other situations where he almost died and miraculously came through. It was a win/win situation for him. He ended up with the better win this time. One of the times he was in the hospital they had lost him but were able to revive him again. When they did, he was extremely upset. I believe he got a glimpse of where he was heading—Heaven—and then to be pulled back into this weak and painful situation, I imagine was too much.

Other than that experience, he remained peaceful through-out this battle and he kept his sense of humor. His true godly character shined. And the grace of God was on him. I know that God's grace was on me, too, during that time. His grace is sufficient; it strengthens and helps us, especially in those kinds of situations. (2 Corinthians 12:9.)

## It's Only Temporary

There were two big things that the Lord did for me to help stabilize me through this. The first one was when I was sitting by my dad's side just days before he died. I had been reading different scriptures to him and was about to read Psalm 116, but then I remembered that verse 15 says, "Precious in the sight of the Lord is the death of His saints" (KJV). I did not want to read that to him for obvious reasons.

Interestingly, a little later as I was sitting there, I sensed the presence of the Lord, and it seemed like, supernaturally, I was aware of anticipation coming from Him. It was the same kind of anticipation that we, as parents, have when we find the perfect gift for our child—one that we know is more than they ever wanted and we become so anxious to give it to them. On a couple occasions, my husband could not even wait to wrap the gift that we had bought for one of our kids. He would just come hurrying out of the room with a blanket over it. My dad had overcome many obstacles in his life and always remained faithful (I'm not saying he was perfect. He just stuck to the path). I believe the Lord was excited about giving my dad all that He had prepared for him in Heaven. This experience and impression that I had didn't last very long. It left me as I was fighting to keep my dad here, but shortly after he died it came back to me, and it brought much comfort.

The other experience that helped me was just as impacting. One day as I was praying and asking for more strength to get through this, all of a sudden the realization of what Jesus did on the cross for us became more real and appreciated than ever before. As I began understanding more clearly the truth that my dad was home safe and has received his ultimate victory because of the sacrifice of Jesus and His resurrection, all I could do was drop to my knees and worship God. I can't describe this experience well enough except that I was flooded with overwhelming gratitude and relief.

We always want what's best for our loved ones. This was the absolute best. Not that we want all our loved ones to go on to Heaven yet, because being here is not only needful for the lost, but it also gives us the opportunity to lay up treasures for there. (Matthew 6:20.) And that I know my dad did. But when they've lived a long life and are ready to go, we can be assured that we'll never have to be concerned about them again. The separation part is what's so hard on us, but thank God that it's only temporary. Paul talks about it in these passages.

**1 Thessalonians 4:13–17 KJV**

13  I would not have you to be ignorant, brethren, concerning them which are asleep, that ye sorrow not, even as others which have no hope.

14  For if we believe that Jesus died and rose again, even so them also which sleep in Jesus will God bring with him.

15  For this we say unto you by the word of the Lord, that we which are alive and remain unto the coming of the Lord shall not prevent them which are asleep.

16  For the Lord himself shall descend from heaven with a shout, with the voice of the archangel, and with the trump of God: and the dead in Christ shall rise first:

17 Then we which are alive and remain shall be caught up together with them in the clouds to meet the Lord in the air: and so shall we ever be with the Lord.

2 Corinthians 4:17,18

17 For our light affliction, which is but for a moment, is working for us a far more exceeding and eternal weight of glory,

18 while we do not look at the things which are seen, but at the things which are not seen. For the things which are seen are temporary, but the things which are not seen are eternal.

Physically, we see our loved ones gone. That's temporary. We can't see them right now, physically existing in Heaven. That's eternal. This goes with any kind of affliction we see going on. It's only temporary. The glory that follows, although we aren't able to see it yet, is indeed eternal. That's where we have to keep our focus.

## Experience Abundant Life

It most definitely does not end with what we now have and get to experience in Christ, here on earth. Paul made that clear when he said, "If in this life only we have hope in Christ, we are of all men most miserable" (1 Corinthians 15:19 KJV).

Before Jesus was taken up into Heaven, He gave us a glimpse of the eternal.

John 14:1–3

1 Let not your heart be troubled; you believe in God, believe also in Me.

2 In My Father's house are many mansions; if it were not so, I would have told you. I go to prepare a place for you.

3 And if I go and prepare a place for you, I will come again, and receive you to Myself; that where I am, there you may be also.

When it was time for Jesus to go up to Heaven, after His resurrection, He began to ascend, as His disciples were watching Him, and He vanished into a cloud. Then something else eternally significant happened.

**Acts 1:10,11**

10 While they looked steadfastly toward heaven as He went up, behold, two men stood by them in white apparel,

11 who also said, "Men of Galilee, why do you stand gazing up into heaven? This same Jesus, who was taken up from you into heaven, will so come in like manner as you saw Him go into heaven."

James, the brother of Jesus and author of the book of James, also talked about Jesus coming back.

**James 5:7,8**

7 Be patient, brethren, until the coming of the Lord. See how the farmer waits for the precious fruit of the earth, waiting patiently for it until it receives the early and latter rain.

8 You also be patient. Establish your hearts, for the coming of the Lord is at hand.

Another time, before Jesus ascended to Heaven, He talked of His return to earth:

**Mark 13:32,33**

32 Of that day and hour no one knows, not even the angels in heaven, nor the Son, but only the Father.

33 Take heed, watch and pray; for you do not know when the time is.

Jesus *is* returning! He is coming back for those who are ready, who have made Him the Lord of their lives. The Word tells us that part of staying ready is to keep watching, keep our hearts ready through prayer. Stay alert and aware of the fact that it could be today. Keep that mindset daily. Don't let it grow old just because you haven't seen it yet, as in the example Jesus gave of an unfaithful servant who lived recklessly because he didn't believe his master would return soon.

Luke 12:45,46 KJV

45 If that servant say in his heart, My lord delayeth his coming; and shall begin to beat the menservants and maidens, and to eat and drink, and to be drunken;

46 the lord of that servant will come in a day when he looketh not for him, and at an hour when he is not aware, and will cut him in sunder, and will appoint him his portion with the unbelievers.

This is talking of the people who don't care about a relationship with the Lord, choosing not to truly let Him be the master of their lives. They're purposely doing whatever they want, believing they will get away with it, because in their minds they think they will have some sort of warning so that they can make it right at the last minute. That's definitely the most dangerous game to play.

Luke 12:39,40

39 Know this, that if the master of the house had known what hour the thief would come, he would have watched and not allowed his house to be broken into.

40 Therefore you also be ready, for the Son of man is coming at an hour you do not expect.

Each day we are literally closer to the second coming of Jesus. Stay on guard, as you would if you were in a security position. Always aware and looking out for anything suspicious. Yet, not just standing idle waiting, but on the contrary, staying busy with the things that really count. Things like growing closer in your relationship with Jesus, and maturing in Him by obeying His Word; looking for opportunities to increase the gifts God has placed in you, by learning more about them and putting them to use. We can see in Proverbs 18:16—"A man's gift makes room for him, and brings him before great men"— that great opportunities will open up for our gifts to be used. We just have to look for them and step into them. We should also be studying how Jesus lived, according to the Gospels, and practice imitating Him.

Hebrews 12:1–4 KJV

1 Wherefore seeing we also are compassed about with so great a cloud of witnesses, let us lay aside every weight, and the sin which doth so easily beset us, and let us run with patience the race that is set before us,

2 looking unto Jesus the author and finisher of our faith; who for the joy that was set before him endured the cross, despising the shame, and is set down at the right hand of the throne of God.

3 For consider him that endured such contradiction of sinners against himself, lest ye be wearied and faint in your minds.

4 Ye have not yet resisted unto blood, striving against sin.

The flesh part of us may have been ruined when sin entered into the world through Adam and Eve giving into temptation

(Genesis 3), but thankfully we won't have to deal with this flesh nature forever. In Heaven we will have new, eternal glorified bodies.

**Philippians 3:20,21**

20 Our citizenship is in heaven, from which we also eagerly wait for the Savior, the Lord Jesus Christ,

21 who will transform our lowly body that it may be conformed to His glorious body, according to the working by which He is able even to subdue all things to Himself.

**1 Corinthians 15:52,53 NLT**

52 It will happen in a moment, in the blink of an eye, when the last trumpet is blown. For when the trumpet sounds, those who have died will be raised to live forever. And we who are living will also be transformed.

53 For our dying bodies must be transformed into bodies that will never die; our mortal bodies must be transformed into immortal bodies.

Once we're aware of these things, we're able to wait in hope and expectation.

**Romans 8:22,23**

22 For we know that the whole creation groans and labors with birth pangs together until now.

23 Not only that, but we also who have the firstfruits of the Spirit, even we ourselves groan within ourselves, eagerly waiting for the adoption, the redemption of our body.

During this stage of hoping and expecting, we have so much to rejoice about because of Jesus and what He did for us. As you're staying ready for His return, seek to learn more about the benefits He's given us,[12] and then share what you learn. That's when you will truly experience the abundant life Jesus came to give us.

# CHAPTER 16

# The Masterpiece of You!

At times, it can seem like this flesh versus spirit battle is constant and never-ending. I hope that this book has helped you to realize that you can win and the how-tos involved. If you'll put into practice what we've been talking about, hold on to your faith and your confession, and cast not away your confidence, I believe that you *will* rise to the top and see the rewards of it. Your spiritual growth will be evident to all and you will make a difference in this world.

Reaching out to others with the good news of the gospel is our purpose for still being here once we are born again. The more you get your eyes off of the battle and on to making a difference in people's lives, the easier and more fulfilling your life will be. Don't dwell on the circumstances, the losses, the disappointments. God promises that they will not last. (2 Corinthians 4:17–18.) You've got to dwell on the outcome that you read in the Word, even though you may not see it yet. God's promises last forever.

One thing the Word assures us of is that this flesh and spirit warfare will eventually cease. When it does, we'll see that the glory far outweighs the hardships. So, hang on and endure to the end. (Mark 13:13.) It's not as far away as you think.

To *endure* is to sustain without breaking; to remain undestroyed, persist, continue in existence, to last; to remain staunch, unmoved in the face of trial, pain, and strain. Here's another scripture that talks about endurance, instructing us what to do:

**2 Timothy 2:3,4**

**3 Endure hardship as a good soldier of Jesus Christ.**

**4 No one engaged in warfare entangles himself with the affairs of this life, that he may please him who enlisted him as a soldier.**

Abraham shows us a great example of endurance. He was given a promise by God that he would have a son. Although he was way too old for that to happen in the natural (so was his wife, Sarah) and it took a while before it did happen, he held on tightly to that promise and believed God against all opposition. (Romans 4:19–20; Hebrews 6:13–14.) Eventually it came to pass: "After he had patiently *endured*, he obtained the promise" (Hebrews 6:15).

Another great example is Moses. Through God's divine orchestration, Moses had been raised in the palace by the daughter of Pharaoh. Yet when Moses was a grown man, he chose to give up his royal position and lifestyle to serve God:

**Hebrews 11:25–27 KJV**

**25 Choosing rather to suffer affliction with the people of God, than to enjoy the pleasures of sin for a season;**

**26 esteeming the reproach of Christ greater riches than the treasures in Egypt: for he had respect unto the recompense of the reward.**

**27 By faith he forsook Egypt, not fearing the wrath of the king: for he *endured*, as seeing him who is invisible.**

Abraham and Moses were able to endure because they believed what God had promised them was theirs.

It takes faith to endure—faith to know that the things that are trying to stop you are neither lasting nor comparable to the reward of enduring to the end, having faith to see the end result, and having faith to look on the One you cannot see with your natural eyes, but you know that He is with you and you will see Him. As Romans 12:3 says, we all have been given a measure of faith. We've just got to build it up and guard it as a most precious jewel.

There are many more Bible examples of people of great faith and endurance, but the best by far is the example of Jesus enduring the cross. We discussed earlier what Jesus went through, but the Word also tells us to consider Him, and the opposition He was up against, when we need strength to endure "lest ye be wearied and faint in your minds" (Hebrews 12:3 KJV). Being diligent to endure and walk by faith is rewarding.

**Hebrews 6:11,12**

**11 We desire that each one of you show the same diligence to the full assurance of hope until the end,**

**12 that you do not become sluggish, but imitate those who through faith and patience inherit the promises.**

It's not possible to follow or "imitate" these examples through weakness and laziness. It takes diligence (or passion and persistence) and strength. We all who are born again have this ability within us.

## Live a Victorious Life

We need to get to the place where we say, "Ok, I cannot accomplish this in my own strength. I've got to take time every day to gain strength from the Lord." It should be a top priority, which is why there's a lot of repetition throughout this book about consistently spending time with God by reading the Bible, praying, praising and worshiping Him, and praying in the Spirit. This is the most important key in living a victorious life, next to obeying the Word of God. Devoting time with the Lord will help you to obey Him. So, these things are worth repeating.

Even Peter saw the importance of continuously reminding the believers of the truth in the Word.

**2 Peter 1:12,13**

**12 For this reason I will not be negligent to remind you always of these things, though you know and are established in the present truth.**

**13 Yes, I think it is right, as long as I am in this tent, to stir you up by reminding you.**

He's saying that it's necessary as long as he is alive in his body to stir them (and us) up by repeating himself to make sure that these important principles will not be forgotten.

A word of caution on this: Don't keep your focus totally on how well you are lining up personally with these truths, or on your own spiritual growth. If all you're concerned about is your own perfection, then you might as well move on up to Heaven where that goal will once and for all be reached. We absolutely need to strive for it, but we've also got to focus outwardly and remember why we're really here.

1 Corinthians 5:9–11

9 I wrote to you in my epistle not to keep company with sexually immoral people.

10 Yet I certainly did not mean with the sexually immoral people of this world, or with the covetous, or extortioners, or idolaters, since then you would need to go out of the world.

11 But now I have written to you not to keep company with anyone named a brother, who is sexually immoral, or covetous, or an idolater, or a reviler, or a drunkard, or an extortioner—not even to eat with such a person.

This scripture passage is talking about how we should not hang around with Christians who are living immoral lives, but we are not supposed to shun the world that's living like that. We've got to try to help them (unbelievers) out of that and show them there's a better way. This is the only reason to go around them, however. It's never to bond with them, to fulfill a need for a close friendship. Paul told us to do just the opposite:

2 Corinthians 6:14

14 "Do not be unequally yoked together with unbelievers. For what fellowship has righteousness with lawlessness [unrighteousness]? And what communion has light with darkness?"

Ephesians 5:11,12

11 Have no fellowship with the unfruitful works of darkness, but rather expose them.

12 For it is shameful even to speak of those things which are done by them in secret.

This Ephesians 5 passage is one more important truth that bears repeating. It gives another good reason why we should really consider what kind of movies and other forms of entertainment we are taking in, as we talked about earlier.

## Finding Personal Satisfaction

Be careful, also, not to do what some Christians do and be extreme in keeping separate from others. They can get so self-absorbed that they want to keep themselves in a bubble to make their own little heaven and not let any evil around them ruin it. We can't ever let that become our issue. Remember, we have a mission here, and it is winning the lost, encouraging and helping other believers, and sharing the love of God everywhere we go.

We are God's ambassadors. (2 Corinthians 5:20.) Personal satisfaction is found when we start looking out for others and quit searching to satisfy ourselves, and when we quit allowing our thoughts, good or bad, to be centered on ourselves—thoughts like, "Woe is me," or "I'm so amazing!"

**Philippians 2:5–7 KJV**
5  Let this mind be in you, which was also in Christ Jesus:
6  who, being in the form of God, thought it not robbery to be equal with God:
7  but made himself of no reputation, and took upon him the form of a servant, and was made in the likeness of men.

Jesus knew His standing with God. He was confident in who He was. But His purpose was not to show that off, although He had every right to. He chose to put that aside and become a servant for our sakes. And that's the way we need to think of ourselves—staying confident of who we are in Christ, yet by choice remaining humble and serving for the sake of Jesus and others.

Ephesians 2:6 tells us that God "raised us up together, and made us sit together in heavenly places in Christ Jesus" (KJV). We're obviously not there physically, but we have been put there spiritually. Things are never as bad as they appear when you're looking down from that view. Insults and rejection from others don't seem to affect you so much when you are secure in your position with Almighty God. You'll see it as wasted time to even defend yourself.

Keeping this all in the right balance and actually doing what you were meant to do will bring true spiritual growth and fulfillment.

## You Are God's Masterpiece

God wants you to always keep in mind how special and valuable you are to Him. Remember, He is faithful and He will finish the work that He started in you. (Philippians 1:6.) Just like a potter works his clay into something beautiful, we are the work of God's hand. (Isaiah 64:8.)

**Jeremiah 18:4–6**

4 The vessel that he made of clay was marred in the hand of the potter; so he made it again into another vessel, as it seemed good to the potter to make.

5 Then the word of the LORD CAME TO ME, SAYING:

6 "O HOUSE OF ISRAEL, CAN I NOT DO WITH YOU AS THIS POTTER?" SAYS THE LORD. "LOOK, AS THE CLAY IS IN THE POTTER'S HAND, SO ARE YOU IN MY HAND, O HOUSE OF ISRAEL!"

Your past mistakes may have seemed to mar your "vessel," but God is saying here that He can remake your vessel (your life) into the masterpiece it was designed to be.

You just have to remain on the wheel (in His presence).

Keep your eyes on the prize and live only in the present, like it's your last day here on earth. And do not let the ugly things that arise from your flesh dictate you. Be quick to shut your flesh down and let the *real you* shine!

# Endnotes

1   Thayer and Smith, *The KJV New Testament Greek Lexicon*, "Greek Lexicon entry for Parrhesia," available from http://www.biblestudytools.com/lexicons/greek/kjv/parrhesia.html, s.v. "confidence," Hebrews 10:35.

2   Based on information from Brown, Driver, Briggs, and Gesenius, *The KJV Old Testament Hebrew Lexicon,* "Hebrew Lexicon entry for Qavah," available from http://www.biblestudytools.com/lexicons/hebrew/kjv/qavah.html, s.v. "wait," Psalm 37:34.

3   See John 14:16,26; 15:26; 16:13.

4   *Albert Barnes Notes on the Whole Bible*, available from http://www.studylight.org/com/bnb/view.cgi?bk=49&ch=4, s.v. "moderation," Philippians 4:5.

5   Based on information from Jameison, Fausset, Brown, available from http://www.biblestudytools.com/commentaries/jamieson-fausset-brown/matthew/matthew-4.html, s.v. "First Stage: he was afterward an hungered," Matthew 4:2.

6   *Adam Clarke's Commentary on the Bible*, available from http://www.studylight.org/com/acc/view.cgi?bk=59&ch=5, s.v. "Verse 8, Seeking whom he may devour," 1 Peter 5:8.

7   Based on information from Adam Clarke, available from http://www.studylight.org/com/acc/view.cgi?bk=44&ch=12, s.v. "Verse 2, By the renewing of your mind," Romans 12:2.

8   Once we are born again, according to Bible commentator Albert Barnes, we are sanctified or are "being made holy; and the idea is, that we become in fact the chosen or elect of God *by a work of the Spirit on our hearts making us holy*; that is, renewing us in the divine image. We are chosen by the Father, but it is necessary that the heart should be renewed and made holy by a work of grace, in order that we may actually become His chosen people." Albert Barnes, available from http://www.studylight.org/com/bnb/view.cgi?bk=59&ch=1, s.v. "Verse 2, Through sanctification of the Spirit," 1 Peter 1:2.

9   Thayer and Smith, "Greek Lexicon entry for Enduo," available from http://www.biblestudytools.com/lexicons/greek/kjv/enduo.html, s.v. "put on," Ephesians 4:24.

10  *The People's New Testament* Bible commentary (1891) by B. W. Johnson, available from https://www.biblestudytools.com/commentaries/peoples-new-testament, Romans 13:14.

11  To crucify our flesh is "to subdue; . . . to destroy the power or ruling influence of." Noah Webster, *American Dictionary of the English Language,* 1828 Edition, available from http://www.webstersdictionary1828.com/Home?word=Crucify, s.v. "crucify."

12  Deuteronomy 28:1–13, Psalm 103, and John 10:10 are just some of the verses that tell us about the benefits Jesus has given us.

# NOTES

# NOTES